Dr. Jim's elementary math prescriptions

This book is part of the **Goodyear Series in Education**,
Theodore W. Hipple, University of Florida, Editor.

OTHER GOODYEAR BOOKS IN SCIENCE, MATH, & SOCIAL STUDIES

**THE CHALLENGE OF TEACHING SOCIAL STUDIES
IN THE ELEMENTARY SCHOOL**
Dorothy J. Skeel

EARTHPEOPLE ACTIVITY BOOK
People, Places, Pleasures and Other Delights
Joe Abruscato and Jack Hassard

ECONOMY SIZE
Carol Katzman and Joyce King

LEARNING TO THINK AND CHOOSE
Decision-Making Episodes for the Middle Grades
J. Doyle Casteel

LOVING AND BEYOND
Science Teaching for the Humanistic Classroom
Joe Abruscato and Jack Hassard

MAINSTREAMING SCIENCE AND MATHEMATICS
Special Ideas and Activities for the Whole Class
Charles R. Coble, Paul B. Hounshell, Anne H. Adams

MATHMATTERS
Randall Souviney, Tamara Keyser, Alan Sarver

THE OTHER SIDE OF THE REPORT CARD
A How-to-Do-It Program for Affective Education
Larry Chase

SELF-SCIENCE
Karen F. Stone and Harold Q. Dillehunt

THE WHOLE COSMOS CATALOG OF SCIENCE ACTIVITIES
For Kids of All Ages
Joe Abruscato and Jack Hassard

For information about these, or Goodyear books in Language Arts, Reading,
General Methods, and Centers, write to

Janet Jackson
Goodyear Publishing Company
1640 Fifth Street
Santa Monica, CA 90401
(213) 393-6731

Dr. Jim's ELEMENTARY MATH PRESCRIPTIONS

Dr. James L. Overholt

*Department of Education
California State University, Chico
Chico, California 95929*

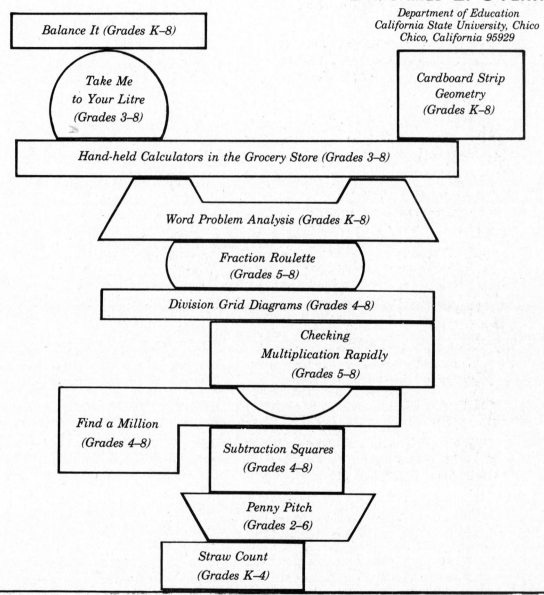

Balance It (Grades K–8)

Take Me to Your Litre (Grades 3–8)

Cardboard Strip Geometry (Grades K–8)

Hand-held Calculators in the Grocery Store (Grades 3–8)

Word Problem Analysis (Grades K–8)

Fraction Roulette (Grades 5–8)

Division Grid Diagrams (Grades 4–8)

Checking Multiplication Rapidly (Grades 5–8)

Find a Million (Grades 4–8)

Subtraction Squares (Grades 4–8)

Penny Pitch (Grades 2–6)

Straw Count (Grades K–4)

ACTIVITIES—AIDS—GAMES TO HELP CHILDREN LEARN ELEMENTARY MATHEMATICS

Goodyear Publishing Company, Inc.
Santa Monica, California

Library of Congress Cataloging in Publication Data

Overholt, James L
 Dr. Jim's elementary math prescriptions.

 Includes bibliographical references and index.
 1. Mathematics—Study and teaching (Elementary)
I. Title. II. Title: Elementary math prescriptions.
QA135.5.093   372.7   78-2013
ISBN 0-87620-225-3
ISBN 0-87620-224-5 pbk.

Library of Congress Catalog Card Number:
ISBN: 0-87620-225-3 (C)
      0-87620-224-5 (P)

Current Printing (last number) 10 9 8 7 6 5 4 3 2 1

Printed in the United States of America

dedicated to Pat, Sara, and Dan

CONTENTS

◉◉◉◉◉◉◉◉◉◉◉

◉◉◉◉◉◉◉◉◉◉◉◉◉◉◉◉◉◉◉◉◉◉◉◉◉◉◉

preface

Teaching elementary mathematics presents a challenge to the conscientious teacher. He or she must have at hand a number of effective methods for helping students understand concepts as well as other methods that provide drill and practice without leading to boredom. Furthermore, it must be decided whether such learning is best accomplished by students at an abstract level or whether pictorial or manipulative tasks would be more appropriate.

Students, on the other hand, do best what they are good at. They don't mind working hard if they understand what they are learning; and if it can be fun, that is even better.

The purposes of this book are (1) to provide a variety of activities that will help students gain competence in working with basic mathematical concepts, and (2) to make sure that these same activities will be enjoyable. The beginning activities dealing with each concept have been presented in manipulative or pictorial fashion. These, in turn, are followed by related activities that will help the students to deal with the concept in an abstract manner. Thus, teachers who utilize these activities will be providing students with alternative means for understanding and appreciating elementary mathematics.

acknowledgments

I wish to thank the many students, teachers, colleagues, and others who directly or indirectly contributed ideas for mathematics activities, aids, or games. I hope the ideas I have selected will make the study of elementary mathematics both better understood and more enjoyable.

As readers review the selections listed in this book, they will no doubt find a number of new ideas as well as some adaptations that have been in use for many years. Since I do not know where certain of these adaptations originated, I am, therefore, unable to give credit.

I was granted a leave from regular duties at California State University, Chico, during the spring of 1977 in order to complete this book. For that opportunity a special note of appreciation is extended. A special thank-you is also conveyed to Kathleen Lewis and Shannon Horn who typed the manuscript.

iNTRODUCTiON

This book is designed for preservice and in-service teachers who wish to utilize carefully selected activities, aids, and games to augment their elementary mathematics programs. The ideas and suggested methods have been tried by teachers and students from kindergarten through grade 8. Some have been useful when working with groups of students, others are learning-center tasks, still others for individualized learning, while many have been used in all of these formats. Thus, this book presents a number of alternatives that the teacher may present to students for learning and practicing elementary mathematics.

To be included, each aid, activity, or game had to meet the following criteria:

1. It had to have a definite purpose within the elementary mathematics program.
2. It had to be enjoyable for students.
3. Any required materials had to be free or inexpensive, and all preparations had to be simple.

Other considerations for selecting activities revolved around the fact that the majority of a student's time in elementary mathematics is spent learning and working with numbers and their basic operations. Thus, Chapters I to VIII deal with those number and operation skills. Chapter IX focuses on the related problem-solving skills; and since hand-held calculators are becoming increasingly more important, some suggestions for their use are described in Chapter X. Basic geometry and measurement-concept development and skill activities are set forth in Chapters XI and XII. Each of the activities is then keyed according to grade level and activity type in the Index (Appendix A).

Each of the chapters begins with concept-building activities that utilize manipulative or pictorial tasks. These are followed by a series of practice activities that students find exciting even though many of the activities require a good deal of concentration and work. For each activity the purpose(s), necessary preparation, directions, and some of the possible variations are noted. It should also be noted that the directions incorporate suggested methods for the teacher to use when introducing and teaching or overseeing the specified activity. Furthermore, all references to he or she within directions were simply assigned to alternate activities; thus, any specific activity might be mastered by either female or male participants. Finally, an asterisk appears in those activities that have reproducible items found in Appendix B.

Learning elementary mathematical concepts and practicing them for mastery can be hard work for students. However, if they understand what it is that they are supposed to learn, and if much of the mastery practice is enjoyable, they can and will develop competence in and an appreciation for mathematics. If the aids, activities, and games suggested on the following pages can help teachers or parents to achieve these goals, then my purpose will have been achieved.

CHAPTER I

NUMBERS AND COUNTING

◎◉◎◉◎◉◎◉◎◉◎◉◎

A child learns to cope with mathematics very early in life. If given a choice, even at two or three years of age, a child would rather have *three* cookies than *one*. He would prefer to have *more than one* piece of candy. Through experiences he has begun to deal with number and counting concepts.

Before long the child discovers that he must use words to ask for what he wants. If he wants *two* popsicles, one for his friend plus one for himself, he must express himself clearly and precisely. His first attempts at counting and relating the appropriate numbers may be accomplished in a rote fashion. As he progresses, however, he soon comes to realize that some numbers tell how many (cardinal numbers) and others tell position or order (ordinal numbers).

A child is generally most able to learn and retain concepts relating to numbers and counting if he must take part in activities that require him to manipulate or picture objects as he tells about the numbers that relate to them. Thus, all but one of the activities selected for this chapter make use of manipulative or pictorial exercises. The activities are also ordered according to level of difficulty, with those involving easier tasks coming first.

The opening activity, titled Straw Count, makes use of plastic drinking straws to show relationships between abstract numbers and objects. Primary Dominoes will, as a follow-up activity, help young students to understand numeral values as they relate to pictorial representations. These two activities should provide a basis for initial number and counting hands-on exercises. The creative teacher may then adapt these ideas to other classroom and playground situations.

◎◉◎◉◎◉◎◉◎◉◎◉◎◉◎◉◎◉◎◉◎◉◎◉◎◉◎◉◎

1

Ideas for using objects to teach and reinforce number combinations are set forth in the activities titled Clothespin Cards, Noisy Boxes, and the Egg Carton Math. Then, as soon as students have mastered most of the basic number facts, they may practice them by using a Math Ball or the Box Puzzles.

Activities, aids, or games from other chapters of this book might also be modified to help the child learn number and counting concepts. Some of these are Mini Place Value Puzzles from Chapter II, Addition Bead Cards and Spill a Sum in Chapter III, Bean Toss Subtraction and Math Jigsaw Puzzles in Chapter IV, plus Balance It and Tinfoil Math Boards from Chapter VIII.

STRAW COUNT

(grades k–4)

purposes

To give children concrete experiences in manipulating and counting objects

To provide practice in regrouping numbers and objects

3 straws and 2 straws = ?

preparation

You will need to obtain 300 or more plastic straws (two large boxes) and 100 rubber bands (one box) of varying lengths. Beginning students will need approximately ten straws for manipulation purposes. More advanced students working together will need up to 100 or 200 plastic straws and some rubber bands to assist them.

directions

Give a beginning student a small number of straws—perhaps five. Then ask him to put three in one group and two in another. If he can do so, then ask him what the total amount is when 3 straws and 2 straws are combined. If he answers correctly, discuss other groupings such as 4 and 1, 5 and 0, 1 and 2 and 2.

A more advanced student might be given seven straws and eight straws and asked to find the total. When doing so, he should be asked to wrap each group of ten straws with a rubber band. This process should be continued until the student has the idea of grouping by 10 firmly in mind.

$$7 \quad + \quad 8 \quad = 10 + 5 = 15$$

variations

The concept of grouping could also be applied, for demonstration purposes, to problems involving more than 100. For example, 87 + 46 = ? could be shown as eight bundles of 10 and seven single straws combined with four bundles of 10 and six singles. Then, using a large rubber band, ten of the bundles would be fastened together to equal 100. The remaining two bundles of 10 and thirteen single straws should also be regrouped into three bundles of 10 and three 1s. Thus, the result would be one bundle of 100 plus three bundles of 10s and three 1s, or 100 + 30 + 3 = 133.

3

primary dominoes
(grades k–3)

purposes

To develop skill in counting pictorial representations

To enforce the ability to match numerals with the corresponding representations

preparation

Construct large dominoes (2" × 4" or larger) with poster board. With a marking pen put a numeral on one end of each domino and a different "pictorial number" on the other.

directions

Have the students each select five dominoes and instruct them to match each numeral with the corresponding picture in the same fashion as a standard domino game. The dominoes are played one at a time, but if a child cannot play she must draw from the remaining dominoes until she can. The child who uses up her dominoes first wins.

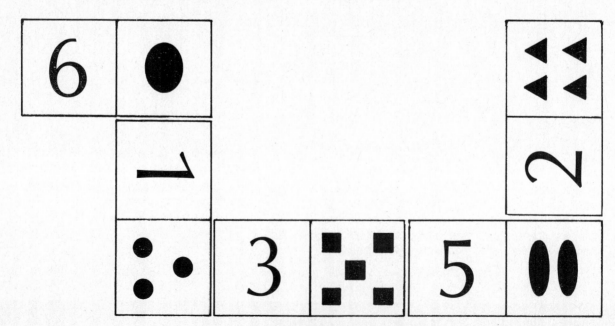

variations

Many kindergarten children very likely would need help to put the dominoes in the right places. As such the game would simply be to match numerals and pictures without applying the domino rules.

For more adept students and for those at upper-grade levels, the game could be adapted for addition, subtraction, multiplication, division, or fractions. To illustrate:

7	4×9	36	4$\overline{16}$	4	6+6	12	15-7

clothespin cards
(grades k–3)

purposes

To give children concrete experiences with basic number facts

To reinforce addition and subtraction number combinations and their reverses

preparation

A supply of 5" × 8" index cards (heavy stock as tagboard or cardboard is even more durable), spring-type clothespins, and a marking pen will be needed. On each card write a numeral, spell out the number name, and put in the appropriate number of dots.

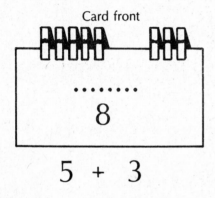

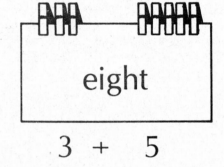

directions

Ask the student to put the correct number of clothespins on the card. In the example above, he could match one clothespin to each dot if necessary. Then ask him to find a combination that equals 8, whereby his response might be 5 + 3 = 8. Also instruct him to turn the card over in order to determine another combination related to the first—namely, 3 + 5 = 8. The student should then continue until he has determined all of the combinations for the number being considered.

variations

The clothespin card process can be utilized for determining or "proving" solutions to many problems. For example, if
$$13 + \underline{\ ?\ } = 21,$$ then:

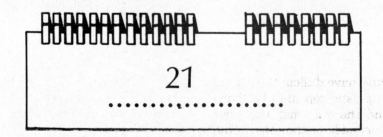

6

noisy boxes
(grades k–3)

purposes

To provide children with a visual (or concrete) aid that will help them to determine basic number combinations

To practice addition and subtraction facts

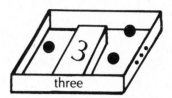

preparation

Obtain ten stationery or greeting card boxes (with plastic lids), forty-five marbles, and ten pieces of Styrofoam or sponge that can be trimmed to fit inside the boxes. Cut the Styrofoam to the shape of a divider (see illustration below) and glue it to the box bottom. Use a marking pen to write the numeral on the divider and the appropriate number of dots as well as the number word on the outside of the box. Finally, insert the correct number of marbles and tape the top on. Make Noisy Boxes for the numerals 0–9.

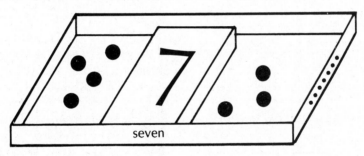

directions

As the student tips or shakes the Noisy Box, the marbles will roll past the divider, thereby giving different combinations that total the same numeral. Then instruct the student to write all of the combinations—for example, with the 7 Noisy Box (shown above) she would find:

4 and 3 = 7	0 and 7 = 7		7 − 0 = 7	7 − 4 = 3
3 and 4 = 7	2 and 5 = 7		7 − 1 = 6	7 − 5 = 2
5 and 2 = 7	1 and 6 = 7	or	7 − 2 = 5	7 − 6 = 1
6 and 1 = 7	7 and 0 = 7		7 − 3 = 4	7 − 7 = 0

variations

If the student should have difficulty with such combinations, the plastic top may be temporarily removed and she may manually move the marbles from one side to the other. Thus, she may also have concrete experiences with all possible combinations for the number/numeral being considered.

EGG CARTON MATH

(grades k–8)

purposes

To develop skills in matching numbers of objects with corresponding numerals

To help determine solutions for number combinations and basic computation problems

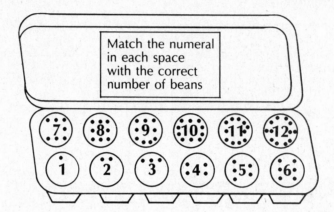

preparation

Obtain a supply of egg cartons (Styrofoam type) and approximately 80 dried beans (or other small markers) to be used with each. Use a marking pen to write the numerals 1 through 12 in each egg space (see illustration above); and, if desired, the appropriate number of dots might also be marked in each space. Also write directions on index cards (see examples in the illustrations) and place these, as they are appropriate, inside the egg carton lid. Furthermore, you may wish to supply scrap paper which the students can tear into approximately 1 inch answer squares. Finally, the egg cartons may be made sturdier and more attractive if the outside portions are covered with decorative Contac paper.

directions

Egg Carton Math may be adapted to mathematical procedures ranging from counting and basic number combinations to multiplication and division. Furthermore, these procedures may be accomplished through manipulation (with beans), by pictorial representations (on the paper scraps), or with numerals.

For counting purposes a student should be asked to match the numeral in each egg space with the correct number of beans. Thus, in the 1 space he would insert one bean, in the 2 space he would place two beans, etc.

To determine number combinations, another student might be asked to place, for example, eight beans in the 8 space of the egg carton. Then she should be asked to redistribute those eight beans into all possible two numeral combinations that are equivalent to 8. Thus, she would determine 7+1 and 1+7, 6+2 and 2+6,

counting to 5

8

5+3 and 3+5 (shown), as well as 4+4 are all equivalent to 8.

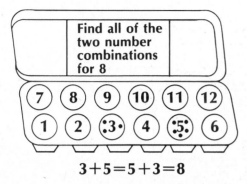

$$3+5=5+3=8$$

For addition the instruction card might tell the student to add 2 to each of the numerals shown in the egg spaces. Then write equations (problems) to show what you found. The same process works in reverse for subtraction. Thus,

if 3 is to be subtracted from the numerals 12 to 3, the result would be 12–3=9, 11–3=8, ... 3–3=0. Furthermore, once a student has attained sufficient understanding, either addi-

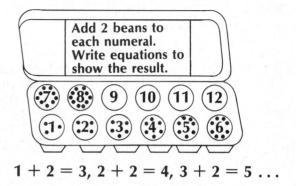

$$1 + 2 = 3, 2 + 2 = 4, 3 + 2 = 5 \ldots$$

tion or subtraction might be completed with pictorial illustrations or with numerals on scraps of paper that are placed in the appropriate numeral spaces (see illustration below).

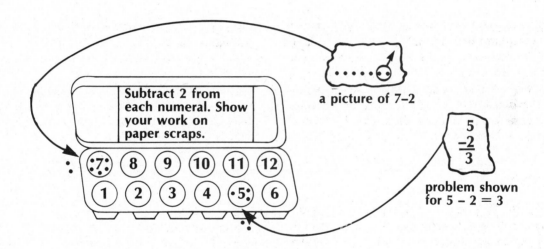

a picture of 7–2

problem shown for 5 – 2 = 3

variations

Multiplication facts can be demonstrated in an egg carton by inserting the proper number of beans into designated number of egg spaces as indicated in an equation. For example, if 9×3 is the problem, we would fill the egg spaces 1 through 9 with 3 beans each for a total of 27 beans in all.

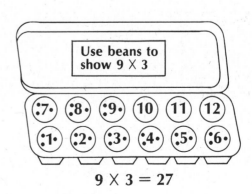

$$9 \times 3 = 27$$

Division, on the other hand, would be dealt with by the distribution of beans into the egg spaces according to the number designated to be in each group. For example, with 18÷3 a student would distribute 3 beans into each egg space beginning with space 1. When finished, egg spaces 1 through 6 would each contain 3 beans; thus, 18÷3=6.

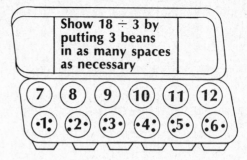

Show 18 ÷ 3 by putting 3 beans in as many spaces as necessary

MATH bALL

(grades k–8)

purposes

To identify the numerals 0–9 and indicate the "how manyness" or cardinality of specific numerals

To practice basic computation

preparation

You will need a rubber ball that students can hold or catch in one hand and that bounces readily. Mark the ball into ten sections with a marking pen and put a single numeral (0–9) in each section.

Thumb at 4

Index finger at 9; little finger at 2

directions

A lower-grade student using the Math Ball might catch it and name the numeral where her thumb (right thumb if two hands are used) is touching the ball. If it is at 4, then she would be asked to bounce the ball exactly four times.

Addition or subtraction might also be accomplished by having the student determine the sum or difference of two numbers touched by her fingers. For example, if the index and little finger are designated and are touching 2 and 9, then $2 + 9 = 11$ or $9 - 2 = 7$. If desired, the answer could again be bounced.

In fact, multiplication and division as well as a combination of computation processes could be done by many upper-grade students. If the student is to accomplish addition, subtraction, multiplication, and division for the numerals touched by all five fingers, the problem might be $5 + 6 - 2 \times 7 \div 4$, $6 + 7 - 2 \times 4 \div 5$, or

whichever arrangement would yield the greatest or least answer as required.

11

variation might involve ordinal as well as
ardinal counting. For example, the student
might touch 3 on the Math Ball with her little
finger. She would then bounce the ball three
times and walk to the third square (the squares
might be temporarily made of tape or perma-
nently painted on the floor).

A different type of variation would be to use
a sponge-rubber ball and to require the student
to catch it in one hand. If she does so, the points
scored for that turn would be the sum (or product) of those touched by any two fingers, provided she gives the correct answer.

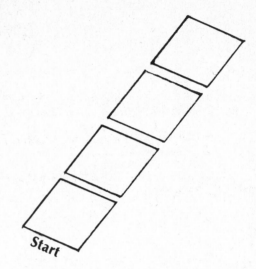

Start

box puzzles

(grades k–8)

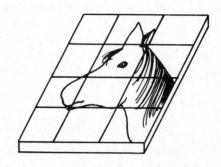

purposes

To develop skills in matching equivalent amounts

To provide practice in basic computational skills

To allow for immediate checking by the student

preparation

You will need one flat box with top and bottom sections (a ditto master box works well), one picture that can fit snugly in the lid of the box, tagboard, glue, scissors, and a ruler. Construct the puzzle as follows:

1. Cut the tagboard so that it will fit inside the box lid.
2. Glue the picture to the tagboard.
3. Rule the back side of the tagboard picture

into squares or other desired shapes.
4. Rule the bottom side of the box into squares or shapes exactly like the tagboard.
5. Write an equation in each of the shapes on the back side of the tagboard picture and the answers in the corresponding shape on the bottom of the box.
6. Cut the tagboard picture into the shapes that have been drawn.

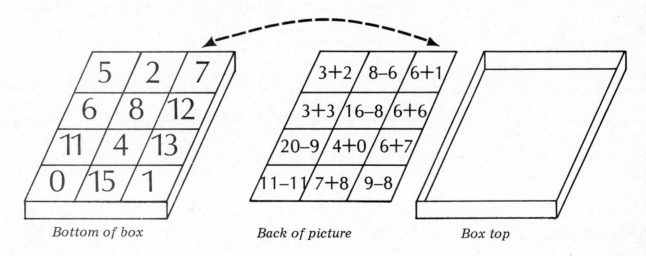

Bottom of box   Back of picture   Box top

Directions

The student puts the equation puzzle pieces on top of the correct answers (equation side up). When all squares are completely filled, the box top is inverted and put over the box bottom (which remains upside down). Hold the box and puzzle pieces together firmly and turn the box

over. Remove the box bottom and look at the picture. If all of the puzzle pieces are in the correct locations, the equations have been answered correctly; if not, those pieces out of order are incorrect and the problems on them should be practiced by the student.

13

variations

A series of Box Puzzles could be used for extra practice at almost any point in a mathematics continuum. To illustrate, they might be used for matching:

1. Number pictures and numerals as [⚫⚫⚫] and [3] .

2. Fractions and representations as [$\frac{3}{4}$] and [◕] .

3. Word problems and solutions (as appropriate).

4. Geometry symbols and names as [↗] and [angle] .

5. Measurement equivalents as [•—•] and [3 cm] .
   (A metric ruler would be needed.)

CHAPTER II

PLACE VALUE

◉◉◉◉◉◉◉◉◉◉◉◉◉◉◉◉

A student should understand the ideas of base and place value before being formally introduced to addition, subtraction, multiplication, and division on whole numbers. To gain a *firm* understanding of these concepts, the student needs numerous manipulative and pictorial experiences in grouping single objects into sets of ten and then with grouping sets of ten to form a hundred.

The first write-up in this chapter, Straw Trading, describes an activity that is best utilized with manipulatives, but it can also be played in pictorial or abstract fashion. It is followed by Mini Place Value Puzzles, which provide for the matching of pictorial and abstract place value representations.

The Place Value War card game and the Place Value Trip, which is played on a gameboard, provide for the study and reinforcement of base ten concepts. Find a Million is an activity that allows children to view and work with a million dots as well as a variety of related place value concepts. Finally, the students will enjoy the Millions Race, which reinforces place value and order with large numbers.

In addition to the place value activities described in this chapter, aids and activities from other portions of this book may also be adapted for such purposes. Some of these are Clothespin Cards and the Egg Carton Math from Chapter I, One Thousand and One in Chapter IV, Multiplication Grid Diagrams in Chapter V, as well as Chalkboard Spinner Games and Scramble from Chapter VIII.

◉◉◉◉◉◉◉◉◉◉◉◉◉◉◉◉◉◉◉◉◉◉◉◉

STRAW TRADING
(grades 1–4)

purposes

To develop place value concepts of 1s, 10s, and 100s with concrete materials

To extend students' understanding of place value and regrouping to pictorial and abstract situations

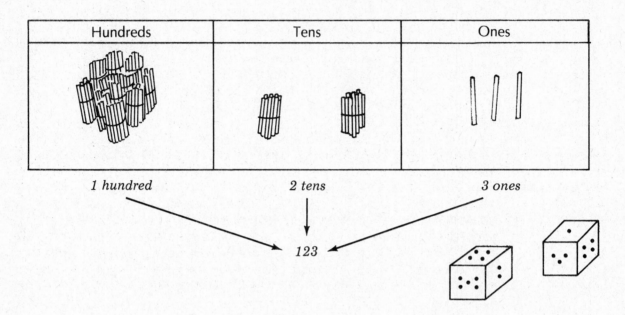

Hundreds	Tens	Ones

1 hundred   *2 tens*   *3 ones*

123

preparation

Materials necessary for Straw Trading are the following:

Plastic straws (200)

Rubber bands (25)

Gameboard or surface (1' X 3')

Marking pen

Dice (2)

Index cards—10 each of three colors (3" X 5")

Construct a Straw Trading gameboard of tagboard (see illustration above) or simply mark it off on a flat playing surface with masking tape. The game surface should be approximately 3

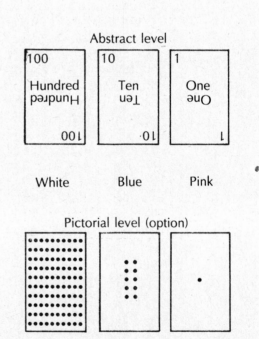

Abstract level

| 100 | 10 | 1 |
| Hundred | Ten | One |

White   Blue   Pink

Pictorial level (option)

16

feet long by 1 foot high; each place value section needs to be about 1 square foot and should be labeled Ones, Tens, or Hundreds, as shown.

Next, label the abstract level index cards as 1s, 10s, and 100s as shown; ten of each will be needed. For certain children the pictorial level cards may also be needed; if so, also label ten each of these.

Finally, be certain that straws, rubber bands, and dice are available.

directions

The Straw Trading game may be played at three levels of difficulty—concrete, pictorial, and abstract. The beginning or concrete level game is played with one student or one team making use of the gameboard, straws, rubber bands, and dice. The dice are thrown. If the sum of the two dice is 8, the student (or team) puts eight straws on the gameboard Ones space. The dice are thrown again. If the sum this time is 9, the student now has eight straws (throw #1) and nine straws (throw #2). At this point he must regroup his 1s into 10s and 1s, or 8 + 9 = 17, which is one 10 and seven 1s. This is done on the gameboard by bundling ten of the straws with a rubber band and placing the bundle in the Tens space while leaving the remaining seven straws in the Ones place. Play continues in this manner until ten 10s have been accumulated. At that point the ten 10s are bundled together with a large rubber band and put into the Hundreds space. The game ends when 100, 200, or any sum designated by the teacher has been achieved.

Once the student readily understands the concepts of 1s, 10s, and 100s with concrete objects (straws), he will be able to move forward to the pictorial or abstract levels. When played at the pictorial level, the cards with dots (see illustration) are substituted for the straws. The dice are thrown, and if the sum is 7, then seven cards with one dot each are placed in the Ones section of the gameboard. The dice are thrown again, and if this second sum is 11, the player now has 11 + 7 = 18. He will then exchange ten of his one-dot cards for a single ten-dot card. The ten-dot card is placed in the Tens section of the gameboard and the remaining one-dot cards are left in the Ones section. Finally, when 10 ten-dot cards are achieved, they are replaced with a single hundred-dot card, which is placed in the Hundreds section. Again, when the desired sum has been achieved, the game is completed.

The abstract level of this Straw Trading game is played in the same manner as the pictorial or dot-card version except that abstract level cards (see illustration) are utilized on the gameboard.

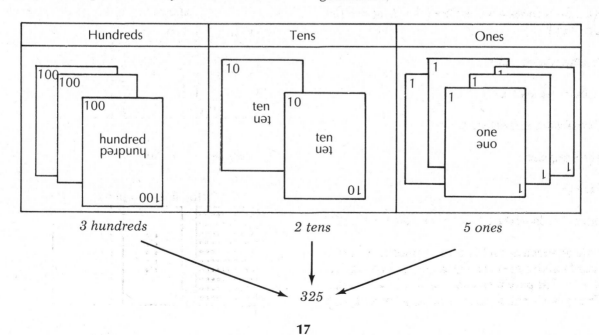

3 hundreds   2 tens   5 ones

325

17

variations

The same gameboard could readily be used with money (play or real)—with pennies as ones, dimes as tens and dollars as hundreds.

It would also be possible to expand the gameboard for use with metric measurement amounts as shown below:

1,000	100	10	1	.1	.01	.001
kilo	hecto	deka	metre	deci	centi	milli

mini pLacE vaLue puzzLes
(grades k–4)

purposes

To develop skill in matching numerals and number pictures with their equivalent place value

To provide for immediate checking by the student

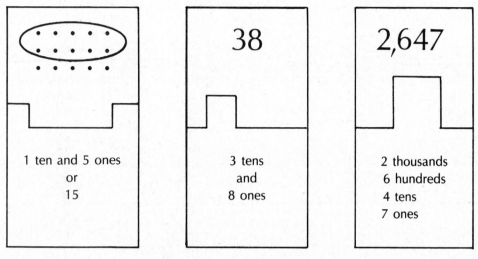

Examples of two-piece puzzles

preparation

You will need poster board (or light cardboard), scissors, and a marking pen. With the marking pen, design individual two- or three-piece puzzles (see illustrations above and below). Be certain that no two puzzles fit together in the same fashion. On one piece of each puzzle, put a numeral or a picture with a number value. On the other, list its place value equivalent. With the scissors, cut all puzzle pieces apart.

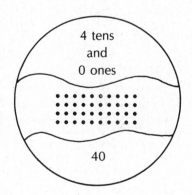

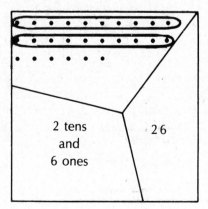

Examples of three-piece puzzles

19

directions

Mix all puzzle pieces together and give them to one student (or a small group). Instruct him to put the puzzles together by matching equivalent amounts. You may want to demonstrate with one puzzle by counting the dots or reading the numeral and discussing why it matches with a certain place value amount. Let the student work by himself, but watch to see which place value amounts he has difficulty with, or ask him to set those pieces aside so that you can help him with them.

variations

Minipuzzles could also be used for numerous other mathematical matching situations including:
1. Dots and numerals such as : and 2.
2. Word problems and answers (as appropriate).
3. Geometric shapes and terms such as □ and square.
4. Computation and answers such as 3 + 2 and 5.

PLACE VALUE WAR
(grades 2–6)

purposes

To provide practice with numerals and their related values

To increase student interest in the place value of numbers

preparation

You will need up to fifty blank cards (or cut 3" X 5" index cards in half with a scissors) and a marking pen. Begin with twenty cards and mark ten with numerals appropriate for your students and the other ten with the correspond-ing place value equivalents as shown in the example above. Later you may wish to increase the deck to thirty, forty, or possibly fifty cards and also make use of place value numerals in the hundreds and thousands.

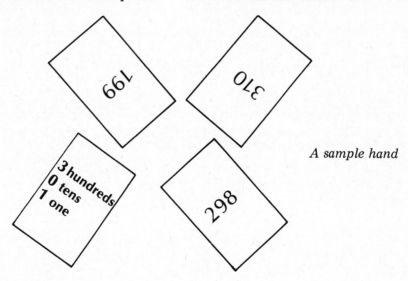

A sample hand

directions

Place Value War is a card game for two to four players. The dealer shuffles and distributes all of the cards face down to the players. Each player should have an equal number of cards.

The players do not look at the cards but rather pile them face down in a stack.

To begin, each player turns her top card over and the one with the "greatest" (or "least") place value wins all the cards shown. These cards are piled separately from the playing cards. This procedure continues, players always drawing from the top, until the stacks are gone. The player with the most cards at the end of the game is the winner.

variations

Remaining in a place value format, the game could be modified to deal with very large or very small amounts. For example:

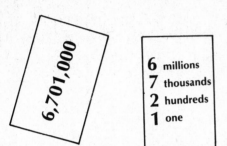

Which is "greater"?

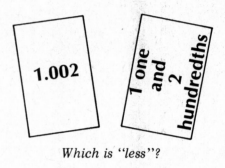

Which is "less"?

The card game can also be played with any of the basic operations in which problems and possible answers are compared. As a sample:

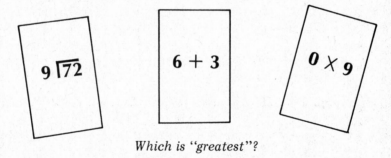

Which is "greatest"?

place value trip

(grades 3–6)

purpose

To reinforce place value concepts

preparation

Obtain a spinner numbered 1–4 (or cards numbered 1–4), markers for individual students, and a piece of tagboard large enough to make a playing board, such as the one shown below.

With a marking pen, divide the gameboard into sections and list place value questions appropriate for your students. Also, insert some "fun" directions in a few of the sections.

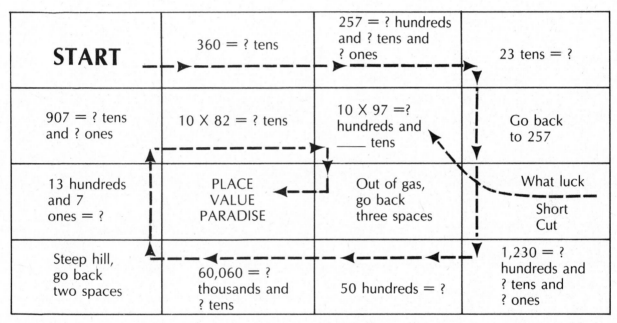

*See Appendix B, Item 1, for a reproducible copy of this Place Value Trip.

directions

To play the game, from one to four students take turns spinning (or drawing cards) to discover the number of spaces to move ahead. If the correct answer is given for the space landed in, the student may stay, but if not, he must go back to the start position. (Or he may opt to keep his marker in the advance square, but when his turn comes again he must give the correct answer for the square previously missed before he can move ahead.) It might also be helpful to keep an answer key nearby in the event of a challenge.

23

variations

When constructing the gameboard you may wish to leave the questions off the board until it has been covered with plastic lamination or clear Contac paper. As such you will be able to change the questions from time to time by simply wiping the board clean and writing in new ones with the proper marking pen.

find A million

(grades 4–8)

purposes

To help students obtain a visual concept of how many a million is

To develop the place value concepts of how many thousands and hundreds there are in a million

To practice reading and computing large numbers

preparation

Prepare a ditto master with about 8,000 dots on it (ditto on next page is 67 × 120 = 8,040). Then run off 130 copies.

directions

Have the students determine how many dots there are on one page. Once they have completed this task, ask how many pages like this it would take to make a million. They might accomplish this via repeated addition, multiplication trial and error, or division. You may wish to allow them the use of a hand-held calculator. Using pages like the sample, it will take about 124½ pages (or 125 pages exactly if there were 8,000 dots per page).

Next, have the students put the pages on a bulletin board, wall, or floor, until they have 124½ pages or a million dots displayed. Now ask how many hundreds there are in a million. Have them mark the dots off a hundred at a time using different colored pens or crayons. When they have solved this problem correctly, then have the students determine how many thousands there are in a million. Complete the same process for tens, ten thousands, etc.

variations

You may use your dots to show everyday data that need to be expressed in large numbers. For example, you might find the dot to show the population of your community, the number of new cars Chevrolet sold last year, etc. Such information can readily be obtained from an almanac or other references.

*See Appendix B, Item 2, for a copy of this Find a Million learning aid that may be reproduced.

millions RACE

purpose

To reinforce place value and order with large numbers

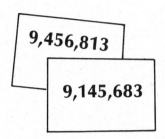

preparation

You will need fourteen 5" X 8" index cards, seven of one color and seven of another. Using a marking pen write a seven-digit numeral such as 9,456,831 on one card in each set. Then on each successive card move the one's digit to the ten's place, hundred's place, etc. To illustrate:

9,456,831	9,451,683	1,945,683
9,456,813	9,415,683	
9,456,183	9,145,683	

directions

Form two teams, each with seven members. Shuffle the cards and give them to the students on each team. At your signal they are to race to the chalk tray where they must line the cards up according to value—lowest to highest. The team finishing first scores 1 point, and each team scores a point for each card that is in the correct order.

9,456,183	9,451,683	9,415,683

variations

Have the teams line up relay fashion and upon signal retrieve designated cards. For example: "Bring back the card which shows four hundred and fifty-one thousands."

A different variation would be to choose a larger number so that more students could participate.

CHAPTER III

addition

◎◎◎◎◎◎◎◎◎◎◎◎

When entering school some children can solve addition problems that are presented orally. However, students generally understand addition best after using simple manipulative and pictorial materials that relate to the problems they are to solve. Such manipulative and pictorial experiences will help to bring about an easier transition to the addition of abstract numbers with less difficulty. Furthermore, such experiences should be followed with abstract number practice activities that students find interesting.

The opening activity in this chapter, Addition Bead Cards, gives children manipulative experiences with basic addition number combinations. It is followed by Spill a Sum, which may be utilized with or without pictorial aids. Further activities including Cover Up, Ping-Pong Throw, and the Penny Pitch each allow an element of chance while at the same time providing practice with addition facts. Elementary logical thinking skills must be utilized as students seek to master Path Boxes, Constructing 3 X 3 Magic Squares, and Add 'Em Up. Finally, the Palindromic Addition process can be set forth as a challenge to intermediate and upper-grade students, particularly those needing remedial assistance with addition operations.

Activities and aids from other chapters of this book might also be readily adapted to help children learn addition. Some of these are Clothespin Cards and the Egg Carton Math from Chapter I, Straw Trading in Chapter II, Bean Toss Subtraction and Subtraction Wheel from Chapter IV, Multiplication Grid Diagrams in Chapter V, as well as nearly all of the Chapter VIII activities.

◎◎◎◎◎◎◎◎◎◎◎◎◎◎◎◎◎◎◎◎◎◎◎◎◎◎◎◎

addition bead cards

(grades k–3)

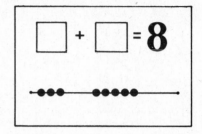

purposes

To give children concrete experiences with basic addition number combinations

To practice writing addition facts

preparation

Obtain fifteen or more tagboard (or heavier material) cards about 5" X 8" in size. With a marking pen write in the numeral, equal sign, addition sign, and blank squares (see illustration). Cover the card with laminating plastic or clear Contac paper. Put the proper number of beads on a string, punch two holes in the card as shown, thread the string through the holes, and tie it on the reverse side.

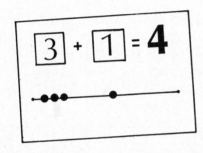

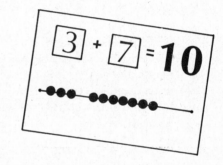

directions

Instruct the student to find as many two-number combinations as he can that will equal the number/numeral on the card. For example, on the number 4 card he should find that 3 + 1, 2 + 2, and 1 + 3 = 4. A beginning student could write each of the number combinations in the blank squares with a grease pencil and have them checked one at a time by the teacher or an aide. A student who works at a more advanced level could write as many combinations as he could find on a piece of paper before consulting an answer key.

variation

Cards of this type could also be used for subtraction. To illustrate subtraction facts associated with 3, the cards might appear as:

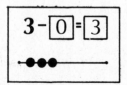
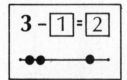
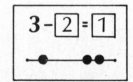

spill A SUM

(grades 1–3)

purpose

To provide practice with basic addition facts

4	1	5
9	7	2
3	8	6

preparation

Rule a cardboard square into nine smaller sections. Number these sections 1–9 in random order. For beginners the same number of dots may also be put into each section. Also, obtain ten dried beans (or other markers) and a small can (or spray can lid).

3	6	8
4	5	1
9	7	2

Game with two beans

7	9	2
6	3	8
5	4	1

Game with six beans

directions

Spill a Sum can be played by two or more students. Each student in turn spills two beans onto the board and adds the sum of those two numbers together. If a bean should fall on a line the student must select just one of those numbers to become part of the sum. If the other players agree with her answer, she scores one point. The game continues until one student has scored ten points or the time is up. The game can also be played using from three to ten beans depending on the ability of the students. If played in this manner, the student must find the sum for all of the numerals which have beans on them.

variations

Spill a Sum could also be played with larger numbers and with zero and negative numbers. As such the game would become useful for upper-grade students.

Another modification would be to play the game for multiplication and title it Spill a Product. Further, it could be played for using all of the basic operations whereby the student would try to achieve a specific answer or come as close to it as possible. For example, if five beans fall on 5, 7, 1, 9, and 2, try to use addition, subtraction, multiplication, and division to equal 2 as $\{[(5 \times 7) + 1] \div 9\} - 2 = 2$.

COVER UP

(grades 1–3)

purpose

To practice various addition combinations for the numbers 2–12

A. | 1 | 2 | 3 | 4 | 5 | 6 | 7 | 8 | 9 | 10 | 11 | 12 |

B. | 1 | 2 | 3 | 4 | 5 | 6 | 7 | 8 | 9 | 10 | 11 | 12 |

C. | 1 | 2 | 3 | 4 | 5 | 6 | 7 | 8 | 9 | 10 | 11 | 12 |

Game	A.	B.	C.	Grand Total
Total				

*See Appendix B, Item 3, for a reproducible Cover Up worksheet.

preparation

Prepare a ditto master, or set of laminated gameboards (see illustration above) so that each student has at least three Cover Up games to play and a grid to record totals and the grand total. Also, have forty or more Cover Up paper or plastic chips (tinted transparent plastic discs are still better since you can see the numerals through them) for each student, and a pair of dice.

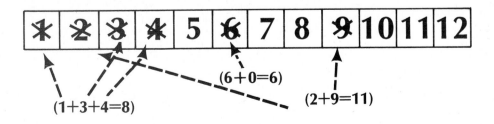

directions

The dice are thrown and two numerals are shown; let us say 5 and 3, which total 8. Each student may then elect to cover up 8 or any combination that makes 8 such as 7 + 1, 6 + 2, or 5 + 3. (A sample Cover Up for one student is illustrated above.) The dice are thrown again and if 4 and 2 totaling 6 results, each student again may choose any combination for 6 to cover up. He cannot, however, use a numeral that was covered on a previous turn. Next, 11 is thrown and the process is repeated. On the fourth dice throw, 5 and 4 for a total of 9 turn up. The game is finished for this student since he has no remaining number combinations that equal 9; however, play continues for the other students. Thus, he must total his uncovered numbers and put the sum in the Total space for Game A (5 + 7 + 8 + 10 + 11 + 12 = 53). At the end of a series of games, the student with the lowest Grand Total is the winner.

variations

Instead of dice, two spinners could be used and any numerals appropriate for the children could be utilized. In fact, by using spinners and more Cover Up numbers, the game could also be played for multiplication.

Spinner Cover Up for 7 × 9 = 63; thus, 63, 60 + 3, 40 + 23, or any such combination could be covered.

pinq-ponq throw

(grades 1–4)

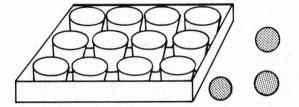

purposes

To provide addition practice and the motivation to accompany it

To help develop fine motor control

preparation

Obtain a shallow box that is approximately 18" × 12" × 3", about forty paper cups, and four or five Ping-Pong balls. With a marking pen write a numeral in the bottom of each cup and then glue the cup to the inside bottom of the box.

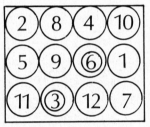

2	8	4	10
5	9	6	1
11	3	12	7

Top view

2	8	4	10
5	9	⑥	1
11	③	12	7

Score of 6 + 3 = 9

directions

A player stands a designated distance back and throws two (or more) Ping-Pong balls into the box of paper cups. She then adds in order to obtain the sum of the numbers where her Ping-Pong balls landed. The player with the largest sum, for that round, receives 1 point (or if the students are able to add larger numbers, they might simply keep a running tally of their raw scores). Play continues for a certain period of time or number of throws and at the end the student with the greatest score is the winner.

variations

When playing the game with two balls, the players may subtract the numbers and the one with the smallest answer wins a point.

Still another adaptation would have the upper-grade students playing the game for multiplication.

35

PENNY PITCH

(grades 2–6)

purpose

To reinforce addition and subtraction skills

preparation

Prepare a dittoed copy of the gameboard for each student like the one shown. (See Appendix B for an enlarged reproducible copy.) Each player will also need a penny or a bottle cap.

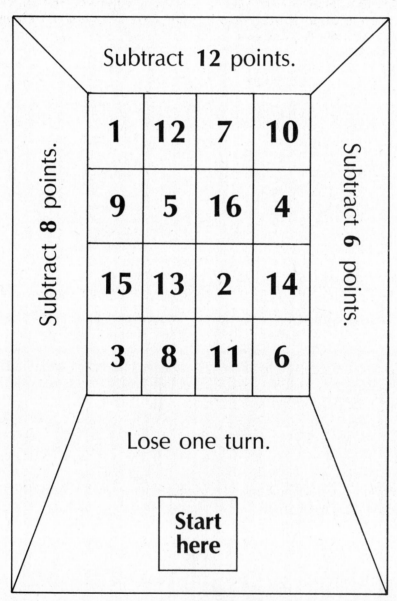

*See Apprendix B, Item 4, for a full page Penny Pitch gameboard that may be reproduced.

directions

Place a penny (or bottle cap) in the Start position. Give the penny a short, quick push. Add or subtract points according to the numeral spaces that the penny is touching. For example, if the penny should land where two lines intersect, those four numbers can be added to your score. The first person to score 100 points wins.

variation

You may also wish to utilize Penny Pitch as a multiplication activity. As such each number the penny touches could be multiplied by a designated factor such as 4. Thus, if the penny lands on 5, the player's score for this turn is $4 \times 5 = 20$, but if the penny touches 2, 6, 14, and 11, his score is $4 \times (2 + 6 + 11 + 14)$ or $4 \times 33 = 132$. As such the first player to reach 1,000 would be designated the winner.

PATH boxes

(grades 2–8)

purposes

To compare addition sums in a logical manner

To provide practice with repeated addition

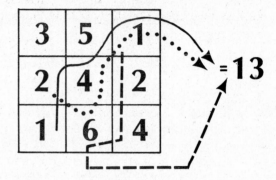

preparation

On the chalkboard (or on ditto) draw an addition Path Box and put a numeral into each section (see illustration). When inserting the numerals, be certain that there is at least one path to the desired sum. It is also helpful to have multiple colors of chalk (or crayons if done on ditto sheets).

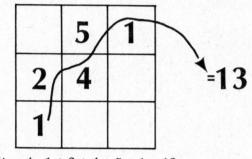

Step A: 1 + 2 + 4 + 5 + 1 = 13

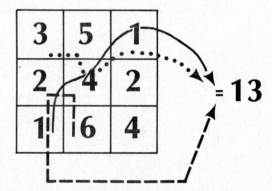

Step B: insert other numerals of similar value

directions

Once the Path Box has been set up, ask the students to find paths to the desired sums, mark them with colored chalk, and write the related addition equation on the chalkboard (or on their papers). See who can obtain the most equations, or the longest equation from the given Path Box.

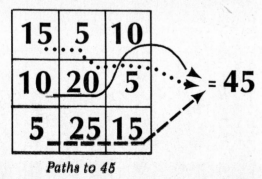

Paths to 45

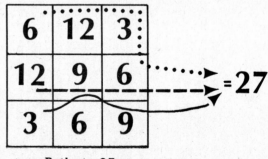

Paths to 27

variations

Path Boxes can be used for combined addition and subtraction equations. In fact, they can also be utilized for multiplication and, in some instances, multiplication and division combined.

CONSTRUCTING 3X3 MAGIC SQUARES

(grades 3–8)

purposes

To reinforce concepts of repeated addition

To provide a system for the immediate checking of answers

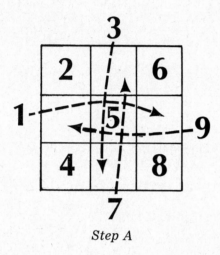

Step A

Magic square with sum = 15

Step B

preparation

Draw a 3 X 3 grid and insert numerals on the diagonal in an evenly spaced sequence as shown in step A above. Next, take the numbers that are displayed outside of the grid and move them as shown. The grid will now appear as in step B above, and it is now a 3 X 3 magic square.

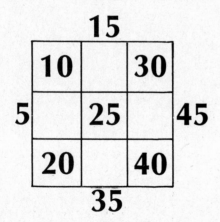

directions

Set up a magic square (on the chalkboard or with pencil and paper) and ask the students to add any three numerals in the square that are in a straight line vertically, horizontally, or diagonally. Have them prove that it is in fact a magic square by adding in all directions (sixteen problems). If their answers are always the same, then their addition computation has been completed correctly. Once they have become proficient at "proving" magic squares, then leave out a number (or two numbers) and have them find out what number it was. On a slightly more difficult level, substitute a numeral that is incorrect and have the students determine which numeral is wrong and what the correct one should be.

If the students become quite adept at "proving" magic squares and with finding missing and incorrect numerals, then show them how to construct magic squares. After they have solved their own and other students' magic squares, let them try them on their parents and friends outside of the classroom.

variations

Have students try very large, very small, fractional, or even negative numbers. Some samples are illustrated below:

2,000	7,000	6,000
9,000	5,000	1,000
4,000	3,000	8,000

Solution = 15,000

.03	.13	.11
.17	.09	.01
.07	.05	.15

Solution = .27

−3	+2	+1
+4	0	−4
−1	−2	+3

Solution = 0

add 'em up

(grades 4–8)

purposes

To practice addition computation

To develop logical thinking skills

preparation

The Add 'Em Up game may be played on a gameboard (also with pencil and paper or as a chalkboard game). The gameboard should be 8" X 8" or larger with a triangle and answer cir- cles (see illustration) drawn in with a marking pen. Nine separate tiles (or bottle caps) numbered 1 to 9 will also be needed.

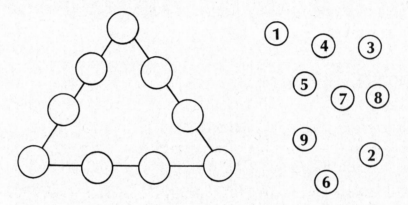

directions

Have each student place all nine of her tiles around the triangle so that each side equals 20 (or 17). After one solution has been determined and the equations recorded, see if another solution can be found.

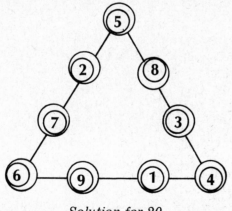

Solution for 20

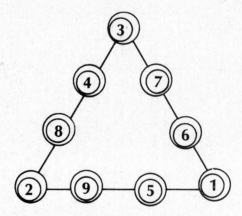

Solution for 17

palindromic addition

(grades 4–8)

purposes

To provide addition practice and challenge for upper-grade students

To provide a means of checking addition competency

$$
\begin{array}{r}
158 \\
+851 \\
\hline
1,009 \\
+9,001 \\
\hline
10,010 \\
+01,001 \\
\hline
11,011 \\
\end{array}
$$

A palindromic or reversible sum

preparation

None. However, a *Guide to Palindromic Sums* for numbers less than 1,000 is provided below and on pages 44 to 45.

directions

Tell the students to take any number less than 1,000 (that is not already palindromic/reversible) and add the number to it that is obtained by reversing its digits. Continue this process for as long as necessary and eventually a sum will be reached that is palindromic (such a number reads the same from either end such as 4,774).

This process is particularly challenging and helpful with upper-grade students who need addition practice, but really don't wish to admit it.

Guide to Palindromic Sums

3 steps

"sum"	*numbers*
11,011	158, 257, 356, 455, 554, 653, 752, 851, 950
13,431	168, 267, 366, 465, 564, 663, 762, 861, 960
15,851	178, 277, 376, 475, 574, 673, 772, 871, 970
3,113	199, 298, 397, 496, 694, 793, 892, 991
5,115	249, 348, 447, 546, 645, 744, 843, 942
5,335	299, 398, 497, 596, 695, 794, 893, 992
6,666	156, 255, 354, 453, 552, 651, 750
8,888	157, 256, 355, 553, 652, 751, 850
6,996	186, 285, 384, 483, 582, 681, 780
7,337	349, 448, 547, 745, 844, 943
7,117	389, 488, 587, 785, 884, 983
7,557	399, 498, 597, 795, 894, 993
9,119	439, 538, 637, 736, 835, 934
9,559	449, 548, 647, 746, 845, 944
9,339	489, 588, 687, 786, 885, 984

Guide to Palindromic Sums (continued)

9,779	499, 598, 697, 796, 895, 994
4,444	155, 254, 452, 551, 650
2,662	164, 263, 362, 461, 560
4,884	165, 264, 462, 561, 660
2,552	184, 283, 382, 481, 580
4,774	185, 284, 482, 581, 680
2,992	194, 293, 392, 491, 590
1,111	59, 68, 86, 95
747	180

4 steps

5,115	174, 273, 372, 471, 570
9,559	175, 274, 472, 571, 670
9,339	195, 294, 492, 591, 690
4,884	69, 78, 87, 96
25,652	539, 638, 836, 935
23,232	579, 678, 876, 975
22,022	599, 698, 896, 995
45,254	629, 728, 827, 926
44,044	649, 748, 847, 946
47,674	679, 778, 877, 976
46,464	699, 798, 897, 996
13,431	183, 381, 480
6,996	192, 291, 390
69,696	729, 927
68,486	749, 947
67,276	769, 967
66,066	789, 987
89,298	819, 918
88,088	839, 938
2,662	280
2,552	290

5 steps

"sum"	*numbers*
79,497	198, 297, 396, 495, 594, 693, 792, 891, 990
45,254	166, 265, 364, 463, 562, 661, 760
44,044	176, 275, 374, 473, 572, 671, 770
59,895	549, 648, 846, 945
99,099	639, 738, 837, 936

6 steps

45,254	182, 281, 380
44,044	79, 97
475,574	779, 977
449,944	799, 997
881,188	889, 988

7 steps

233,332	188, 287, 386, 485, 584, 683, 782, 881, 980
881,188	197, 296, 395, 593, 692, 791, 890
45,254	190

8 steps

    1,136,311   589, 688, 886, 985

      233,332   193, 391, 490

10 steps

    88,555,588   829, 928

11 steps

    88,555,588   167, 266, 365, 563, 662, 761, 860

14 steps

    8,836,886,388   849, 948

15 steps

    8,836,886,388   177, 276, 375, 573, 672, 771, 870

17 steps

    5,233,333,325   739, 937

    133,697,796,331   899, 998

22 steps

    8,813,200,023,188   869, 968

23 steps

    8,813,200,023,188   187, 286, 385, 583, 682, 781, 880

    8,802,236,322,088   879, 978

24 steps

    8,813,200,023,188   89, 98

variations

You might want to challenge the students further by asking them to see who can find a problem that takes the greatest number of steps to achieve a palindromic sum.

Also, for enrichment, the students might be asked to see if they could find a problem that has a palindromic sum of 1,111 (or another designated sum). Perhaps a hand-held calculator could be utilized in this process.

CHAPTER IV

SUBTRACTION

◎◎◎◎◎◎◎◎◎◎◎◎◎◎◎◎◎◎

Subtraction presents a more complex learning situation for children than was encountered with addition. Thus, it is particularly important that students deal with subtraction in pictorial and manipulative situations prior to learning the subtraction facts. Following such activities, motivational subtraction practice, in other than textbook or worksheet formats, should also be set forth for the students. The activities in this chapter do provide selected ways to accomplish such subtraction learnings and reinforcement practice.

Bean Toss Subtraction is an activity which causes students to manipulate selected numbers of beans and then to write the abstract mathematical sentences that correspond to them. It is followed by the Subtraction Wheel that provides students with pictorial experiences in subtraction.

Several of the activities allow for the learning and reinforcement of subtraction facts. They include Math Jigsaw Puzzles, Punch-Out Figures, Touch and Subtract, and Subtraction Ring. These, in turn, are followed by Stay Out of the Hole and One Thousand and One that insert elements of chance and skill into the process. Finally, Subtraction Squares are set forth as a unique method for subtracting either positive or negative numbers.

Activities from other chapters of this book may also be modified for use with subtraction. Some of these are Noisy Boxes and the Egg Carton Math from Chapter I, Addition Bead Cards and Penny Pitch in Chapter III, Pictorial Division from Chapter VI, as well as all of the activities in Chapter VIII.

◎◎◎◎◎◎◎◎◎◎◎◎◎◎◎◎◎◎◎◎◎◎◎◎

bean toss subtraction

(grades k–3)

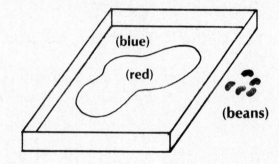

purposes

To give children concrete experiences with basic subtraction number concepts

To provide practice in writing subtraction facts

preparation

Obtain a box lid approximately 9" X 12" X 1" or larger. Inside the lid glue blue paper and on top of it glue a smaller piece of red paper (see illustration). You will also need at least nine dried beans or other markers.

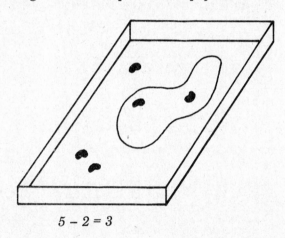

$$5 - 2 = 3$$

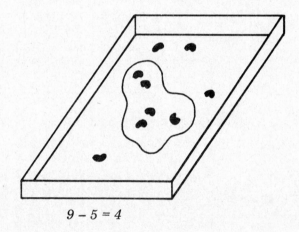

$$9 - 5 = 4$$

directions

Have one student drop or toss a specific number of beans into the box; for example, let us say 5. If, out of 5 beans, 2 land on the red paper then how many are left on the blue paper; that is, $5 - 2 =$ ____. Thus, each student is to set up an equation after the sample: total number of beans minus the beans on the red paper equals the beans remaining on the blue paper; or, in the example noted above, $5 - 2 = 3$. Toss the beans again and see if another equation can be found such as $5 - 0 = 5$, $5 - 1 = 4$, $5 - 3 = 2$, $5 - 4 = 1$, or $5 - 5 = 0$.

If, later on, a student should have difficulty with a problem like $9 - 5 =$ ____ have him take 9 beans and put 5 on the red paper and the remaining beans on the blue. Then let him count the number remaining on the blue paper, or $9 - 5 = 4$. The same procedure may be applied to problems like $35 - 27 =$ ____.

variation

A bean toss type of game could also be used to set up addition equations wherein the situation would become: number of beans on red area plus number of beans on blue paper equals the total number of beans.

subtraction wheel

(grades k–3)

purpose

To provide students with pictorial and abstract experiences for subtraction

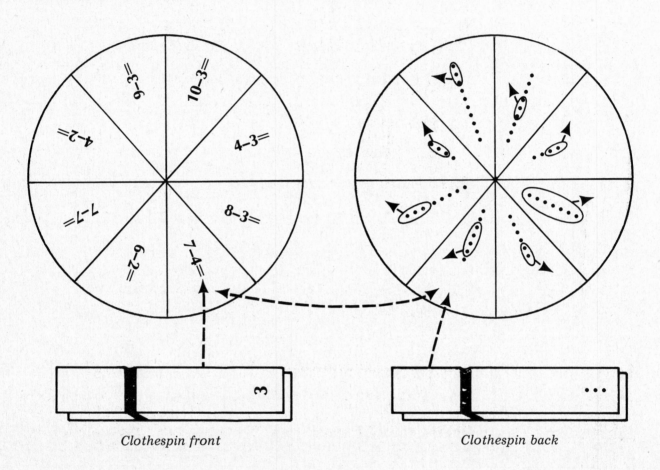

Clothespin front   Clothespin back

preparation

Cut a 6" diameter wheel from tagboard or cardboard. Then mark the front and back of the wheel into eight sections that are the same size and which are located back to back. On the front of the wheel write subtraction equations and on the same section of the back show the problem in pictorial fashion (see illustration; also note that $7 - 4 = $ __?__ and ..⬭. both equal 3).

Next, prepare spring-type clothespins as answer keys. To do so, write an answer for each equation in pictorial fashion on one side of the clothespin and as a numeral on the other.

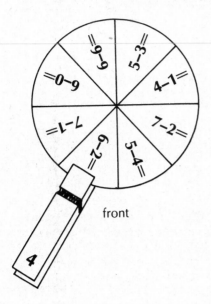

front

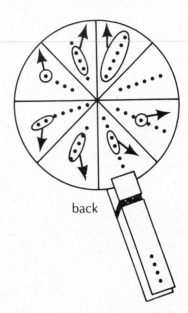

back

directions

Demonstrate for the students how the clothespin Subtraction Wheel works; for example, the 6 – 2 section matches with the 4 clothespin and on the back side of the wheel • • ⊂••⊃➤ matches with the back of the same clothespin where • • • • appears. Then instruct the students to complete the wheel and to check both sides to be certain they are correct.

If you wish to use the wheel as a checking device, simply put in a few extra answer clothespins that do not match the wheel.

variations

The wheel and clothespin procedure could easily be adapted for addition, multiplication, division, or matching fractions.

MATH jiGSAW PUZZLES

(grades k–3)

purposes

To provide motivational practice for subtraction facts and problems

To allow students to check the accuracy of their work immediately

preparation

Obtain (or construct) several frame-type jigsaw puzzles. With a marking pen, trace around each puzzle piece in such a manner that its shape is outlined inside the puzzle frame. Then write subtraction problems on the back side of the puzzle pieces and the corresponding answers in the outlined space within the puzzle frame.

directions

Instruct the student to take all of the pieces out of the puzzle frame, turn them upside down, and mix them up. She should then read each subtraction problem and if she thinks she knows the proper answer, put it into the puzzle frame and see if the puzzle piece matches the shape of the area occupied by the corresponding answer. If the piece matches, she should leave it in place, but, if not, she should set it aside. After matching all problems and answers that she knows she then begins work on any problems that she was not able to answer directly. She does so by putting the puzzle together according to the shape of the piece and the puzzle picture. At the same time she should record the problems that she could not initially answer as well as their corresponding answers (such as $23 - 9 = 14$ or $16 - 7 = 9$) on a sheet of paper.

Having completed the puzzle task, she should then work out the problems missed in a concrete fashion. For example, $23 - 9$ could be done with straws and rubber bands where 23 is represented as two bundles of 10 straws and 3 single straws. The student should then proceed to take 9 straws away by taking the 3 straws and then breaking a bundle of 10 (regrouping or borrowing) and taking 6 more straws for a total of 9. The remaining straws then equal a bundle of 10 and 4 more, or 14. Thus, $23 - 9 = 14$.

variations

Math Jigsaw Puzzles could easily be adapted for addition, multiplication, division, or work with fractions and decimals. Also, the puzzles might be modified to match geometric shapes and terms, word problems and solutions, measurements and equivalent amounts, etc.

PUNCH–OUT figures

(grades 1–4)

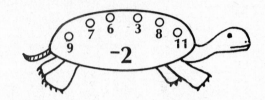

purposes

To reinforce basic subtraction (and addition) concepts

To allow for immediate checking of answers

preparation

You will need a paper punch, scissors, marking pen, and tagboard. Sketch or trace any figure (coloring books can be a good source for animal figures) on the tagboard and cut it out with the scissors. Then use the paper punch to make holes near the edges of the figure (see illustration below). Next, select a series of subtraction problems that need to be practiced and write the minuend (or sum) next to each hole and the subtrahend (or known addend) in the center of the figure with the operation sign in front of it. On the back side of the figure at the corresponding punched hole, write the difference (remainder).

Notice that we may also use the back side of the figure for addition practice. All that is necessary is for the sum to be the same amount as was the minuend on the reverse side.

Front

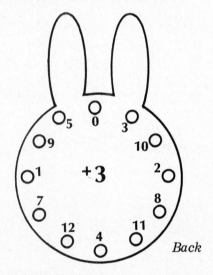

Back

*See Appendix B, Item 5, for a reproducible pattern of the Rabbit Punch-Out Figure.

directions

Direct the student to say or write the answers to each subtraction or addition problem around the figure. As he tries each problem, for example 8 – 3, he puts the point of his pencil through the hole next to the subtrahend (or known addend) and turns the figure over to check his answer. Thus, $8 - 3 = 5$, or from the back side of the figure, $5 + 3 = 8$.

variation

Punch-Out Figures can also be utilized in the same manner for multiplication and division problems.

TOUCH AND SUBTRACT

(grades 1–4)

purpose

To provide practice with basic subtraction facts

*See Appendix B, Item 6, for a reproducible Touch and Subtract gameboard plus answer pieces.

preparation

Obtain a piece of tagboard that is 14" X 14" and mark it into 1" squares. Using a scissors, carefully cut out the gameboard half (see illustration) and, with a marking pen, insert the numerals along the edges. Next, take the leftover tagboard section and cut it into 1" square pieces. Each of these pieces must then be marked with an answer numeral. There needs to be an answer for each blank space on the playing board plus a few empty pieces. Finally, an answer key should also be prepared.

directions

The answer pieces are mixed up and one to four players take ten unseen pieces each. The player with the greatest answer numeral begins by placing that numeral on the gameboard in a proper location. For example, the player with the answer piece 9 might place it at the intersections of 11 and –2 (11 – 2 = 9). (Other possibilities would also have been 10 and –1 or 12 and –3.) The next player must place an answer piece on the gameboard that touches the first player's piece horizontally, vertically, or diagonally such as at 11 and – 3 (11 – 3 = 8). Other players in turn follow the same procedure. However, if at his turn a player does not have an answer piece that can touch a piece already on the board, she may play a blank piece in any touching position; but any other player may replace this blank piece with a correct answer piece at any time. Further, if at her turn a player has no correct answer pieces or blank pieces, she must then draw from the unused pile until she obtains a piece that can be played. Play continues in this manner until one player has placed all of her pieces on the gameboard.

variations

This type of game could be readily adapted for addition or multiplication. With a few further modifications, it could also be used for work with fractions or division.

subtraction ring
(grades 2–6)

purpose

To provide practice with subtraction computation at varying levels of difficulty

preparation

Cut a subtraction ring with an 8" diameter
from tagboard. Separate the ring into sections
and mark each with a numeral. Cut twenty or
more circles with 2" diameters and mark each
of these with numerals 12–99. Also, make an
answer key.

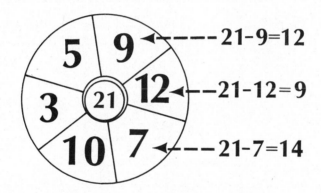

directions

Place the small numeral circles face down and
mix them up. Each player draws a circle, and
the one with the largest numeral plays first. He
puts his numeral circle in the center of the
subtraction ring and subtracts each number on
the ring from the number in the center. The
other players may use the answer key to check
his work if necessary. If he gives all answers
correctly, he keeps his circle, but if not, he returns it face down to the numeral circle pile.
Play continues in this fashion until all of the
cards have been used or a set amount of time
has ended. The winner is the one who has col-
lected the greatest number of numeral circles.

variations

Reverse the process and have the students add
the numbers on the ring to those on the numeral circle in the center.

Also, the ring and circle numerals could be
multiplied or divided by upper-grade students.
Perhaps these answers might be checked with
a hand-held calculator.

STAY OUT Of THE HOLE

(grades 3–8)

purposes

To develop skill in computing repeated subtraction problems

To enhance throwing skills

preparation

You will need a 24" × 24" piece of tagboard or cardboard, a marking pen and ruler, and three bean bags. Rule the tagboard into four-inch squares and write zero or a negative numeral in each.

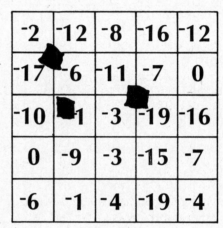

‾2	‾12	‾8	‾16	‾12
‾17	‾6	‾11	‾7	0
‾10	‾1	‾3	‾19	‾16
0	‾9	‾3	‾15	‾7
‾6	‾1	‾4	‾19	‾4

Player 1

‾2	‾12	‾8	‾16	‾12
‾17	‾6	‾11	‾7	0
‾10	‾1	‾3	‾19	‾16
0	‾9	‾3	‾15	‾7
‾6	‾1	‾4	‾19	‾4

Player 2

directions

Allow each player a set number of points to begin the game—let us say 99. Then the student must subtract from that 99 any negative values determined when her three beanbags are thrown onto the game surface. For example, the scores for players 1 and 2 (see examples above) are as follows:

$$
\begin{array}{r}
99 \\
-16 \quad (0, -16) \\
\hline
83 \\
-45 \quad (-15, -19, -7, -4) \\
\hline
38 \\
-16 \quad (-6, 0, -9, -1) \\
\hline
22
\end{array}
$$

Score—Player 1

$$
\begin{array}{r}
99 \\
-37 \quad (-2, -12, -17, -6) \\
\hline
62 \\
-1 \quad (-1) \\
\hline
61 \\
-40 \quad (-11, -7, -19, -3) \\
\hline
21
\end{array}
$$

Score—Player 2

The winner is the player with the largest remainder. However, any player who scores less than zero—goes in the hole—automatically loses regardless of what her opponents' scores may be.

variations

Given a different title, this game could be used for addition or multiplication and the objective would be to achieve the greatest score.

ONE THOUSAND AND ONE

(grades 4–8)

purposes

To provide subtraction computation practice including renaming (borrowing) skills

To develop logical thinking skills

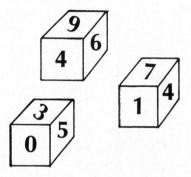

preparation

You will need three blank dice (may be made of sponge or wood cubes) and a marking pen. Write the following numerals on each die with the marking pen:

Die 1 — 0, 1, 2, 3, 4, 5

Die 2 — 1, 3, 2, 6, 4, 7

Die 3 — 4, 5, 6, 7, 8, 9

directions

Have each player roll the three numbered dice and arrange the numerals to make a number. The player then subtracts that number from 1,001. As they take turns, each player may elect to roll 1, 2, or 3 dice and subtract the number from his previous answer. The winner is the player who is nearest to or at zero. However, if anyone goes in the hole (a negative answer), he automatically loses. The following illustrates a game with two players:

	dice numbers		dice numbers
1,001		1,001	
– 810	(0, 1, 8)	– 742	(2, 4, 7)
191		259	
– 96	(6, 9)	– 86	(0, 6, 8)
95		173	
– 93	(3, 9)	– 96	(6, 9)
2	(stop)	77	
		– 62	(2, 6)
		15	
		– 12	(1, 2)
		3	
		– 2	(2)
		1	(winner)

variation

For more adept students larger numbers may be put on the dice. These numbers in turn may be subtracted from 1,000,001 or any other prescribed number.

subtraction squares

(grades 4–8)

purposes

To provide subtraction computation practice for zero, positive, and negative numbers

To motivate reluctant students

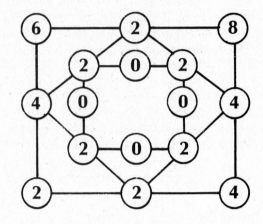

preparation

None is required; however, for some students it might be advisable to have ditted copies of the Subtraction Squares (see example with 16, 2, –11, and 0 as corner numbers) with six or seven squares within the original one.

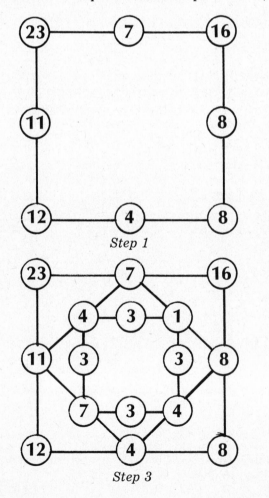

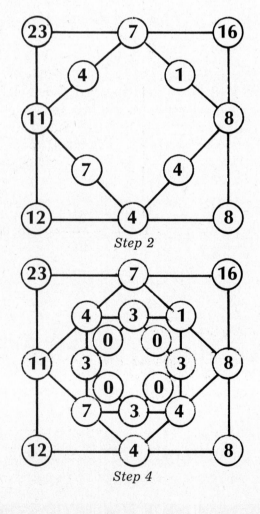

60

directions

Instruct the students to complete the same subtraction square with pencil and paper that you will do on the chalkboard. Let the students select any numbers to put in each corner; perhaps they might choose 23, 16, 8, and 12. Along each line subtract the smaller number from the larger one and write the difference in the circle between them (Step 1). Next, connect those answers with diagonal lines, subtract and insert the new answers in the diagonal line answer circles (Step 2). Connect these new answers,

again vertically and horizontally, and subtract again (Step 3). Continue this process until no further subtracting can be done (Step 4).

After the students have determined that the result of their first Subtraction Square is zero, they will most likely ask whether that will always happen. Suggest that they try it and find out. A word of caution: it is wise to have two or more students work with the same Subtraction Square numbers since, by doing so, they can quickly locate errors, if any.

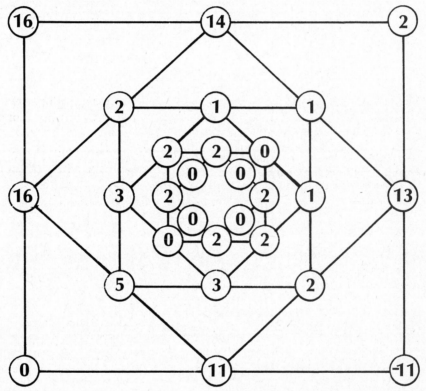

*See Appendix B, Item 7, for a reproducible Subtraction Square or Division Square diagram.

variation

A similar process can also be completed for division. See also "Division Squares."

CHAPTER V

MULTIPLICATION

◎◉◎◉◎◉◎◉◎◉◎◉◎◉◎◉◎◉◎◉◎◉◎

When first learning to multiply, students should have experiences that will help them to understand the process. In most instances multiplication will be taught in terms of equal additions, but in some situations arrays or Cartesian products may also prove helpful. In any case, however, the students should progress to the point of achieving immediate recall of the basic multiplication facts. The activities in this chapter will provide assistance for the teacher as she attempts to help the children learn multiplication.

The initial activity, Multiplication Grid Diagrams, provides a means by which students may construct their own pictures of multiplication. The second write-up, Concentrate on Multiplication, allows for both pictorial and abstract representations of multiplication to be studied.

Two of the activities that make use of logical thinking skills as well as reinforcing multiplication facts are Here I Am and Tangle Tables. Then Multo and Lattice Multiplication provide alternate means for practicing basic facts, whereas Hookey is an activity which coordinates chance and repeated multiplication. The final activity in the chapter, Checking Multiplication Rapidly, provides a quick process for determining the accuracy of multiplication answers.

Activities, aids, and games from other chapters may also be adapted for use with multiplication. Some of these are the Egg Carton Math and Math Ball from Chapter I, Spill a Sum and Penny Pitch in Chapter III, Punch-Out Figures and Touch and Subtract from Chapter IV, Division Factor Puzzles and Division Rummy in Chapter VI, as well as all of the Chapter VIII activities.

◎◉◎◉◎◉◎◉◎◉◎◉◎◉◎◉◎◉◎◉◎◉◎◉◎◉◎

multiplication grid diagrams

(grades 3–8)

purposes

To have students construct their own pictorial diagrams of multiplication

To provide a means for proving multiplication products

preparation

Provide each student with a supply of grid (graph) paper and a pencil or crayon.

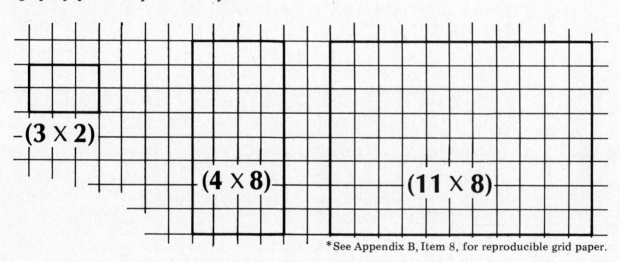

*See Appendix B, Item 8, for reproducible grid paper.

directions

Begin with a simple multiplication fact problem such as 3 × 2 =____ and ask what it equals. If the students know the answer is 6, then ask why is that so. Discuss their responses and ask them if they could draw a picture of the solution. At that time pass out the grid paper and have them draw a line along the border of a rectangle that is 3 units long and 2 units wide (see above). Next, ask the students to find out how many square units are surrounded by this rectangle. Thus, they will determine that 3 × 2 = 6.

Once a student has mastered this basic multiplication concept process, have him do others such as 4 × 8 = 32 (illustrated above). Also note that if the 4 × 8 grid diagram is laid on its side, we can then view 8 × 4 which also equals 32.

The grid diagram procedure can also be utilized for pictorially "proving" the accuracy of any problem. For instance, 11 × 8 = 88 (see above) might be proven by viewing the 11 columns of 8 units each or even by counting all 88 of the units within the figure.

variations

The grid diagram process may be used with basic addition, subtraction, and division. Note also that similar diagrams are also used widely in applied mathematics situations. For example, when designing floor plans, a 9' × 12' room is often mapped out in the same fashion.

CONCENTRATE ON MULTIPLICATION

(grades 3–8)

purposes

To provide multiplication drill and practice

To enhance pictorial and abstract comparisons

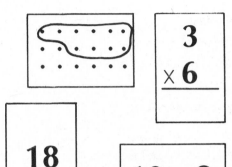

preparation

Index cards (3" × 5") and a marking pen will be needed. Using facts appropriate for your students, prepare four matching cards (see illustration above) for each multiplication fact. In this fashion prepare a deck with from 28–56 cards.

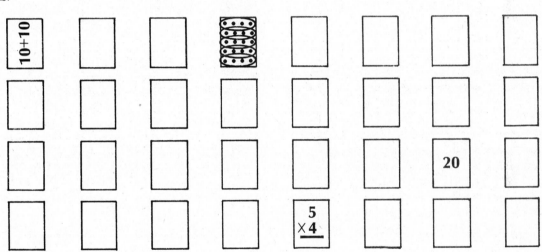

directions

This concentration game may be played by two or more students. The cards are shuffled and placed face down in rows and columns (or a scattered arrangement for greater difficulty). The students then, in sequence, each turn over two cards. If they match in value, the student keeps them and tries again. If they do not match, they are turned over again and the next player tries. Play continues until all of the cards have been removed. The winner is the player with the most cards at the end of the game.

variations

Concentration may be played for addition, subtraction, division, and fraction comparisons. In fact, it may be utilized for any matching situation such as geometric shapes and names, word problems and solutions, etc.

HERE I AM

(grades 4–8)

purposes

To reinforce basic multiplication facts

To stimulate logical thinking

X	1	2	3	4	5	6	7	8	9
1	1	2	3	4	5	6	7	8	9
2	2	4	6	8	10	12	14	16	18
3	3	6	9	12	(H)	18	21	24	27
4	4	8	12	16	(E)	24	28	32	36
5	5	10	15	20	(R)	30	35	40	45
6	6	12	18	24	(E)	36	(I)	48	54
7	7	14	21	28	35	42	49	56	63
8	8	16	24	32	40	48	(A)	64	72
9	9	18	27	36	45	54	63	(M)	81

Master gameboard

preparation

Prepare a "master" multiplication gameboard with answers, and several players' gameboards without answers (see illustrations).

The master gameboard should be at least 10" X 10" with 1" squares, and the student gameboards are to be the same size (or from dittoed copies—four to a page).

Cover the gameboards with a plastic lamination or clear Contac paper (not necessary on student ditto copies since they are disposable after use). Next, use seven paper discs, 1" in diameter, and print on them the individual letters for HERE I AM. Finally, if the students are to use plastic-covered gameboards, they will need grease pencils or marking pens with water-soluble ink.

X	1	2	3	4	5	6	7	8	9
1									
2									
3					×15				
4					×20				
5					×25				
6					×30				
7							49		
8					40				
9									

*See Appendix B, Item 9, for a reproducible Here I Am student gameboard.

directions

The teacher (or leader) places the discs for Here I Am on the master gameboard, being careful to keep their locations secret. The lettered discs may be placed in horizontal, vertical, or diagonal fashion, but the letters of each word must be in adjacent squares and there must be only one space between words.

The game begins when one person calls off a multiplication problem and its correct answer. All players record the answer in the proper grid location. Further, if that multiplication fact matches a grid space on the master gameboard where a lettered disc is located, the teacher (or leader) says "Here I Am," and the students put an "X" on that location. The student tries a second time and if she locates another letter, the leader again says "Here I Am," but if not, the next player tries another multiplication fact. The game proceeds in this manner until one or more students think they know the location of all of the Here I Am discs. They must then call out all of the multiplication fact problems that correctly indicate the disc locations. Any student to do so properly is a winner.

66

The following is an example (using the illustrations on the previous page) of how the game is played. Student A calls out the fact $7 \times 7 = 49$ and the leader says "correct," and all students put the answer on their gameboards. Student B says $3 \times 5 = 15$, and the teacher says "Here I Am." Thus, all students write the 15 and mark it with an "X". Student B then calls out $4 \times 5 = 20$, $5 \times 5 = 25$, and $6 \times 5 = 30$ with each successive turn, and all players mark these answers with "Xs" on their gameboards. Student B then tries $8 \times 5 = 40$, and the leader says only "correct"; thus, Student C now has a turn. The game continues until seven "Xs" are recorded and one or more students are able to correctly call off the multiplication facts for the disc locations.

variations

Here I Am can readily be adapted for addition. It could also be used for subtraction and division. However, when doing so for subtraction, be aware that negative numbers will be necessary, or simply do not use that half of the gameboard. Furthermore, doing division problems on this gameboard would involve remainders or fractional answers.

MULTO
(grades 4–8)

purposes

To reinforce multiplication facts

To provide an element of chance

preparation

Prepare dittoed copies (without numbers) of the grid shown below for all players. Also, have available multiplication flash cards from 1 X 2 to 10 X 10 and a container to draw the cards from. Finally, provide scratch paper that can be torn into approximately 1" squares by the students.

20	9	49	25	42
15	24	18	36	48
5	30	Free	35	8
6	56	54	64	81
9	10	63	40	72

5 x 5

8 x 9

*See Appendix B, Item 10, for a blank reproducible Multo grid.

directions

Distribute Multo dittoed grids to all players. Then direct the players to take part in group practice of a series of multiplication facts. As the players answer the problems aloud, they should write the answers only in any location on their Multo grids. After twenty-four such facts, their Multo grids will be filled.

Now have the students tear their scratch paper into twenty-five 1" squares and place one square over the FREE space on the Multo grid. The teacher (leader) then proceeds to call off the problems (not the answers) that were earlier practiced aloud. If a student knows the answer, he writes the problem on a scratch paper square and places it over the answer (see 5 X 5 and 8 X 9 illustrated above). The winner(s) is the first student(s) to get a complete row or diagonal line covered.

variations

The game can be played for "blackout" where the entire grid must be covered in order to win.

The same game could also be played to reinforce addition, subtraction, or division facts. As such, it might be called "Addio," "Subto," or "Divio."

lattice multiplication
(grades 5–8)

purposes

To provide practice with basic multiplication facts

To enhance success feelings with multiplication, especially for students having difficulties

To provide an alternate means for checking standard multiplication problems

preparation

None.

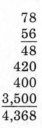

$$
\begin{array}{r}
78 \\
56 \\
\hline
48 \\
420 \\
400 \\
3,500 \\
\hline
4,368
\end{array}
$$

(answer)

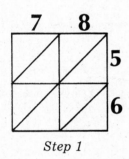

Step 1

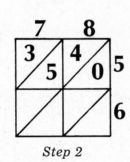

Step 2

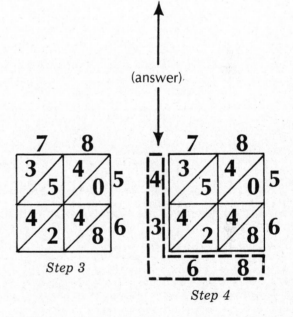

Step 3

Step 4

directions

Lattice Multiplication may be helpful for students encountering difficulties, as enrichment activities for others, and as a means of checking problems completed with a standard algorithm. As you will soon discover, it only requires the student to practice multiplication facts and addition in order to solve problems.

For example, let us assume that a student was not able to solve 56 × 78 (see above) with a standard algorithm. She might then be shown how to construct a 2 by 2 lattice and where to locate the factors 78 and 56 (Step 1). Next 5 ×

8 is multiplied with the aid of a chart if necessary, and 40 is written in with the 4 tens above the lattice line and the 0 ones below it (Step 2); also 5 × 7 = 35 is recorded in the same way. The multiplication facts 6 × 8 = 48 and 6 × 7 = 42 are included in the lower row (Step 3) in the same fashion. Now, all that is necessary is for the student to add (Step 4) on the lattice in order to find the solution. The first lattice (lower right corner below diagonal lattice line) contains only an 8, thus 8 is recorded. The second lattice (read on the diagonal) has 0 + 4 +

2 = 6 and 6 is recorded. Lattice three contains 4 + 5 + 4 = 13; thus, the 3 is written and the 1 is carried to the fourth lattice. Finally, lattice number four includes 3 plus the 1 carried over or 3 + 1 = 4. Reading along the left and lower edges, we find 4,368 to be our solution.

As a further example, another lattice multiplication problem has been completed below. In this example, the student will need to practice multiplying her 7s, 8s, and 9s times 6, 7, 8, and 9.

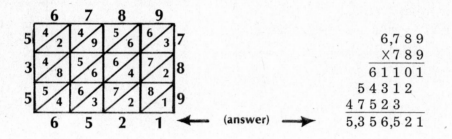

$$\begin{array}{r} 6,789 \\ \times 789 \\ \hline 61101 \\ 54312 \\ 47523 \\ \hline 5,356,521 \end{array}$$

(answer)

TANGLE TABLES

(grades 5–8)

purposes

To give students practice with multiplication facts

To stimulate logical thinking

X				3
	5	0		
4			0	12
	9	54		
		12		6

preparation

Prepare a ditto master with several Tangle Tables and duplicate enough copies for each student. Tangle Tables may be drawn on the master with a pencil and ruler and be any size beginning with a 4 × 4 grid. (A 5 × 5 example is shown above.) Note that a multiplication sign is written in the upper left corner and that the lines down the first column and across the first row are double in order to separate the factors from the products.

The numerals are arranged by writing all factors and products in very lightly and then darkening approximately two factors or products in each row and column. Finally, erase any numerals which should not show.

X					
		12			3
	10		30		
			42		7
		36		72	
				0	

6 × 6 Tangle Table

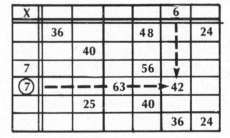

7 × 7 Tangle Table

*See Appendix B, Item 11, for blank reproducible Tangle Tables.

directions

Draw one of the Tangle Tables that appears on the dittoed sheets on the chalkboard (or overhead projector) and begin to work it out with the students. For example, in the 7 × 7 Tangle Table above we see that 6 × ____ = 42. Thus, the missing factor is 7, and we write it in such that the row with 7 and the column with 6 intersect at 42 (shown with dotted arrows). Each of the other multiplication facts are solved in a similar logical fashion until we determine that the numerals in the top row are 6, 5, 9, 8, 6, and 4, and those in the left column are 6, 8, 7, 7, 5, and 6.

71

After the students have worked with several Tangle Tables, they may make their own on graph paper. They may wish to make up a Tangle Table with missing elements and another complete with answers. They can then challenge other students to solve them and retain the completed copy to use later for checking purposes.

hookey

(grades 5–8)

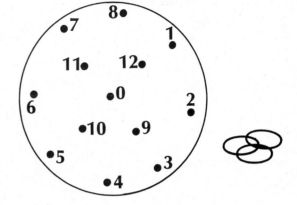

purposes

To give practice with repeated multiplication

To provide for throwing skill practice

preparation

Obtain a circular piece of wood approximately 18" in diameter. Paint or draw thirteen numerals on it (see illustration), and next to each insert an L-shaped nail or cup hook. Also, procure six rubber canning rings (or cut the centers out of plastic coffee can lids).

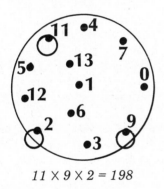

$11 \times 9 \times 2 = 198$

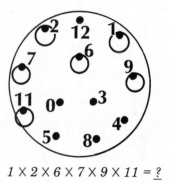

$1 \times 2 \times 6 \times 7 \times 9 \times 11 = \underline{?}$

directions

Each player throws from three to six rings from a specified distance and tries to accumulate the greatest score. Scoring is accomplished by mentally multiplying the "ringed numerals" together (see examples above). The player's mental multiplication is then checked by another player using pencil and paper or a hand-held calculator.

variations

Hookey can be readily adapted for addition practice with or without the aid of pencil and paper.

Another procedure is to allow any operation with the numerals in order to come as close to a specified score as possible. For example, if 50 was designated and 11, 9, 6, and 2 were ringed we might try:

$$[(11 - 6) \times 9] + 2 = 47$$
or
$$[(9 \times 2) - 11] \times 6 = 42$$
or
$$[(9 \times 11) + 6] \div 2 = 52.5$$

73

checking multiplication rapidly

(grades 5–8)

purpose

To give students a quick process for checking multiplication products

preparation

None.

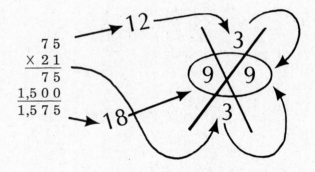

directions

Instruct the students to draw a large X-shaped figure (see illustration above) to one side of a completed multiplication problem. Next, have them add the digits of the multiplicand, being certain to repeatedly add the resulting digits together until the total is less than 10 (thus, 7 + 5 = 12 and 1 + 2 = 3). Place this digit at the top of the X as shown above. Complete the same process with the digits of the multiplier, and place this second digit at the bottom of the X (2 + 1 = 3). Next, multiply the digits at the top and bottom of the X together (3 × 3 = 9), and if necessary reduce that product to a total less than 10 by repeatedly adding the digits together. Place that result at the right side of the X. Finally, add the digits of the original problem's answer together repeatedly until a one-digit total results (1 + 5 + 7 + 5 = 18 and 1 + 8 = 9). Place this new total on the left side of the X. If the left and the right side of the X contain the same numeral (as circled above), then the answer is nearly always correct.

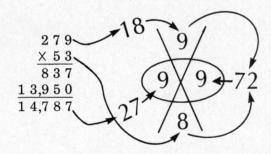

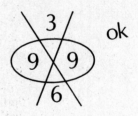

CHAPTER VI

division

◉◎◉◎◉◎◉◎◉◎◉◎◉

When first being introduced to division as a formal process, the students should actually construct sets, equal in number, from a given set. These manipulative activities should soon be followed up by having the students draw their own pictorial representations of division situations. Then, as they come to better understand division, they will need to practice it in a variety of settings. The activities in this chapter will allow students to utilize pictorial representations and to complete division activities in a series of situations.

Pictorial Division is the first activity suggested in this chapter. It provides a process by which students can draw their own pictures of division results. As such, they can actually "prove" their division answers. Division Factor Puzzles and Division Rummy are two alternate activities that provide basic division fact practice. Football Remainders and Divide to Get Home make use of gameboard-type practice with larger division problems, whereas Averaging Activities stipulates division uses from the everyday world. Checking Division Rapidly allows students to quickly determine the accuracy of their answers, and Division Squares affords division practice with decimals as well as whole numbers.

Activities from other chapters may also be modified to provide division learning and practice. Some of these are the Egg Carton Math and Box Puzzles from Chapter I, Punch-Out Figures and Math Jigsaw Puzzles from Chapter IV, Concentrate on Multiplication and Multo in Chapter V, Fraction Roulette and Calculating and Comparing from Chapter VII, as well as most of the activities from Chapter VIII.

◉◎◉◎◉◎◉◎◉◎◉◎◉◎◉◎◉◎◉◎◉◎◉◎◉◎◉◎◉

pictorial division

(grades 4–8)

purposes

To give children a visual concept of division

To provide a means for proving division results in a pictorial fashion

preparation

Provide each student with a supply of grid (graph) paper and a pencil or crayon.

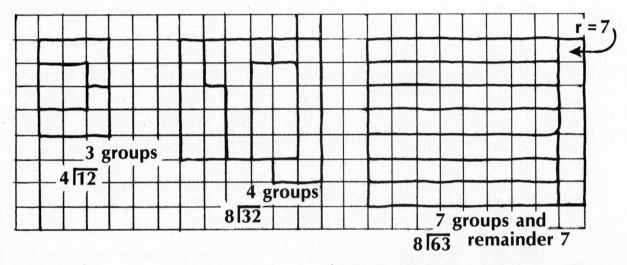

3 groups
4⟌12

4 groups
8⟌32

7 groups and remainder 7
8⟌63

r = 7

*See Appendix B, Item 8, for reproducible grid paper.

directions

Consider a simple division problem such as 12 ÷ 4 = _____ and ask how many groups of 4 make up 12. Suggest that a good picture of the problem might be drawn by enclosing 12 grid squares with a line and then subdividing that space into areas of 4 squares each (see illustration above). Continue by doing similar but in- creasingly more difficult problems like 32 ÷ 8 and 63 ÷ 8.

Such a grid diagraming procedure can also be utilized for pictorially "proving" the accuracy of any problem. On occasion you might also want to use it with larger problems such as 129 ÷ 41 (see below).

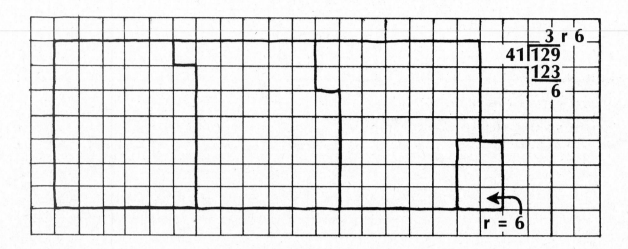

variations

Try using the grid diagram process with addition, subtraction, and multiplication. Also, similar diagrams may be used in applied situations such as in the design of a lawn sprinkling system.

division factor puzzles

(grades 4–8)

purposes

To provide practice with division facts

To allow for immediate checking of results

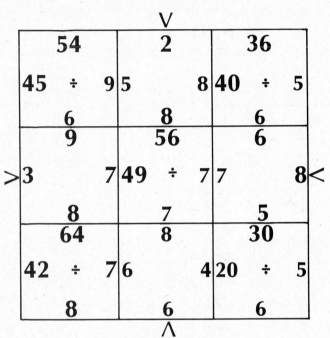

A completed puzzle

preparation

Use a pen and ruler to mark a piece of tagboard into 1" squares, (illustrated is a 3 × 3 factor puzzle). Next, write division fact problems and the corresponding answers in alternate squares. You may also wish to insert random numerals into the outside pieces where no answers would be placed (noted >). Cut out the puzzle pieces in random fashion. (The greater the number of pieces, the more difficult the puzzle becomes.) You may wish to code the back side of the pieces in order to prevent several puzzles from becoming mixed up. Finally, place all of the pieces in an envelope marked according to the total size of the finished puzzle—as 3 × 3 or 5 × 5, etc.

directions

Instruct each student using a Division Factor Puzzle to take the pieces out of the envelope and mix them up. She should then match the factors and answers so that they are aligned vertically and horizontally with the final puzzle being a square or rectangle of the size noted on the envelope.

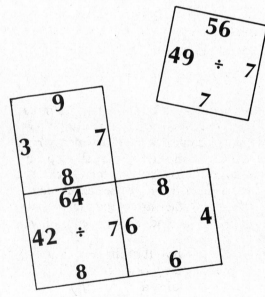

Factor pieces

variations

Factor puzzles have numerous uses. They may be used to match related numerals and answers for addition, subtraction, multiplication, and fractions. They can also be used for equating numerals with their corresponding pictorial representations, and geometric figures with their names.

division RUMMY

(grades 5–8)

purpose

To promote rapid recall of division facts

preparation

Obtain a blank set of fifty playing cards (or cut 3" X 5" index cards in half). Write basic division combinations on twenty-five of them and quotients on the other twenty-five.

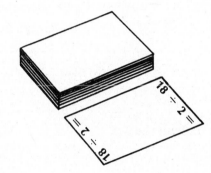

directions

The game is played with two to four students. The dealer shuffles the cards and deals seven to each player. He places the remaining cards face down in a pile and turns over the top card.

Players check their cards for matching division combinations and quotients. All matching pairs are placed face up on the table in front of the player who had them (see illustration above).

The player to the left of the dealer then takes either the turned-up card or draws one from the pile. If he obtains a matching card, he lays the pair down. In any case, he must also discard a card and put it face up beside the pile.

Play continues with the next student to the left repeating the process. Should he want a card below the top one in the discard pile, however, he must take all the cards above it also. The game continues until one player is rid of all his cards.

A point is scored for each matching pair that a student has. The winner is the player with the most points after a given time period or number of rounds.

variations

Rummy can also be played for addition, subtraction, and multiplication combinations and their respective answers.

79

football REMAINdERS

(grades 5–8)

purposes

To reinforce division skills

To encourage accurate and rapid division calculations

preparation

Make a set of cards with the numbers 2–9 written on them and a football marker for each team. A football field, similar to the one shown, may be used as a gameboard or put on the chalkboard.

directions

Football Remainders may be played by two or more students with half being on each team. The number cards are mixed, and each team captain draws a card. The team with the highest numeral will play first beginning at their own 20-yard line.

To begin play the number cards are mixed again, and one card is drawn. The player "carrying the ball" must then divide the 20-yard number by the card number. If he does this properly, he moves ahead the number of spaces (each space is 5 yards) of the remainder. For example, if the player for team one draws the card numbered 9, he then must do $121 \div 9 = 13$, remainder 4. If the other team agrees, he then moves his team's football ahead four spaces or to the 40-yard line (see illustration). However, if he gave an incorrect answer, and this could be shown by the opposing team, he would have to move his team's football marker back that number of spaces. Play now alternates to team two that must divide their 20-yard number by whatever number card they draw.

The game continues in this manner with the members of each team taking turns "carrying the ball." The winning team is the one that makes either the first touchdown or the most touchdowns within a period of time.

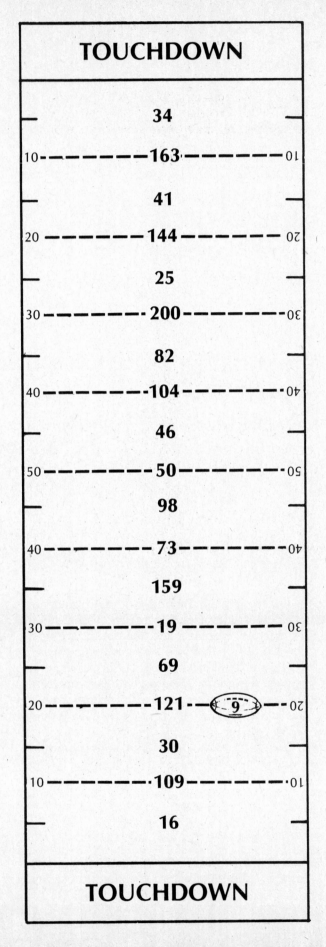

variations

The football approach could also be utilized for addition, subtraction, and multiplication practice. However, the forward and reverse movements would need to be designated in a different manner.

checking division rapidly

(grades 5–8)

purpose

To provide for immediate division reinforcement

$$7\overline{)29}$$
$$\underline{28}$$
$$1$$
with quotient 4

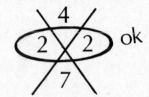

preparation

None.

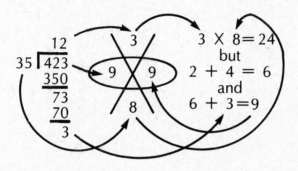

$$35\overline{)423}$$ with quotient 12
$$\underline{350}$$
$$73$$
$$\underline{70}$$
$$3$$

3 × 8 = 24
but
2 + 4 = 6
and
6 + 3 = 9

directions

Instruct the students to draw a large X-shaped figure (see illustrations above) to one side of a completed division problem. Then have them add the digits of the quotient together until their total is less than 10 (1 + 2 = 3) and place this digit at the top of the X. Complete the same process for the digits of the divisor and place this second total at the bottom of the X (3 + 5 = 8). Next, multiply the digits at the top and bottom of the X together and, if necessary, re-

duce that product by repeated addition to a total less than ten (3 × 8 = 24, but 2 + 4 = 6). Also, if there is a remainder, add it to that sum (6 + 3 = 9) and place that amount on the right side of the X. Finally, add the digits of the dividend together until a one-digit total results (4 + 2 + 3 = 9) and place this new total on the left side of the X. If the left and right side of the X contain the same numeral (as circled above), then the answer is nearly always correct.

$$917\overline{)52,612}$$ with quotient 57
$$\underline{45,850}$$
$$6,762$$
$$\underline{6,419}$$
$$343$$

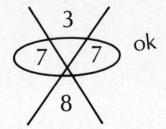

82

divide to get Home

(grades 6–8)

purpose

To provide division computation practice

preparation

On tagboard or cardboard make a gameboard similar to the example shown below. You may want to cover the grid surface with laminating plastic or clear Contac before writing the numerals; by doing so, you can change numbers without having to construct a new board. Also write the numbers 2–9 three times each on twenty-four small cards. Finally, a small gameboard marker is needed for each player.

3,001	366	213	2,331	3,751	112
988	587	123	4,005	612	88
714	1,199	10,100	HOME	399	9,600
659	912	7,891	3,456	401	382
1,112	580	316	6,789	5,112	1,001
2,847	319	812	651	452	Start ★

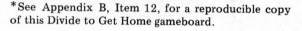

*See Appendix B, Item 12, for a reproducible copy of this Divide to Get Home gameboard.

directions

Divide to Get Home is normally played by two to four students. To start, the cards are mixed and placed in a pile face down. A player turns over the top card and divides the starting number by the card number (452 ÷ 5 is the problem illustrated above). If the player answers correctly at her turn, she can move ahead four spaces, but if not, she must move backward three spaces. An answer key or hand-held calculator may be used to check the student's answers.

The game continues in the same manner, with each player taking turns, until one player reaches home.

variations

The game could also be used for addition, subtraction, or multiplication computation. It might then be entitled "Add to Get Home," etc.

AVERAGING ACTIVITIES

(grades 6–8)

purposes

To help students understand averaging concepts

To practice in applying division skills to everyday situations

preparation

The students will need pencil and paper.

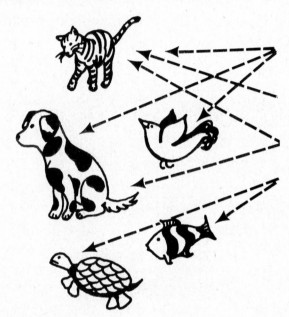

Family A = 3 pets

Family B = 1 pet

Family C = 2 pets

Family D = 2 pets
_____
8 pets total

$$4\text{ families }\overline{\smash{\big)}\,8\text{ pets}}^{\textstyle 2\text{ pets per family}}$$
$$\underline{8}$$

directions

The teacher might begin by asking a leading question, such as, "How many pets do you think each family in our class has?" After some discussion, someone will likely suggest that everyone in the class could be asked how many pets their family has. Now have someone record the responses on the chalkboard (see example above). Notice that some families have as many as three pets each and some have just one pet each. Then ask, "How many pets should I expect to find if I go to a home where I have never been before?" At this point you will need to find the total number of pets and divide it by the number of families. This, of course, will provide an average number of pets you might expect to find in one household.

As the concept of average is developed further, use additional everyday situations such as:

1. What is the average height of five third-grade children? (See example below.)
2. What is the average number of teeth that seventh-grade students have in their mouths?
3. What is the average number of cars per family?
4. What is the average cost of a new car?

84

36
44
48
55
58
241

48⅕ inches is the average height

5 students ⟌ 241 inches
       200
        41
        40
         1

division SQUARES

(grades 7–8)

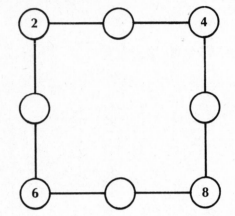

purposes

To provide division practice including decimal computation

To provide a means for students to check their division results

preparation

None is required; however, you may wish to duplicate blank copies of the division squares for each student.

directions

Work out a Division Square with the students. Place any four numbers in the corners of the square (see illustration with 2, 4, 8, and 6 above) and divide the larger number along each line by the smaller and insert the quotient in the answer circle between them. Next, connect those first answers with diagonal lines and again divide the larger number by the smaller, once again putting the answer in between. Repeat the process again along new vertical and horizontal lines. Continue this repeated process until the students are surprised by the quotients all being 1.

When they ask whether the process will always yield an answer of 1, suggest that they try several problems to find out. At this point have at least two students begin with the same num-

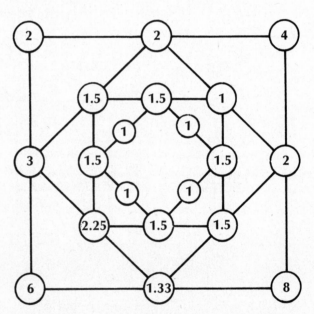

*See Appendix B, Item 7, for a reproducible Division Square or Subtraction Square diagram.

bers; in this way, if an error is made, they can check each other.

Reprinted from the *Arithmetic Teacher,* October 1971 (vol. 18, pp. 402–5), © 1971 by the National Council of Teachers of Mathematics: Used by permission.

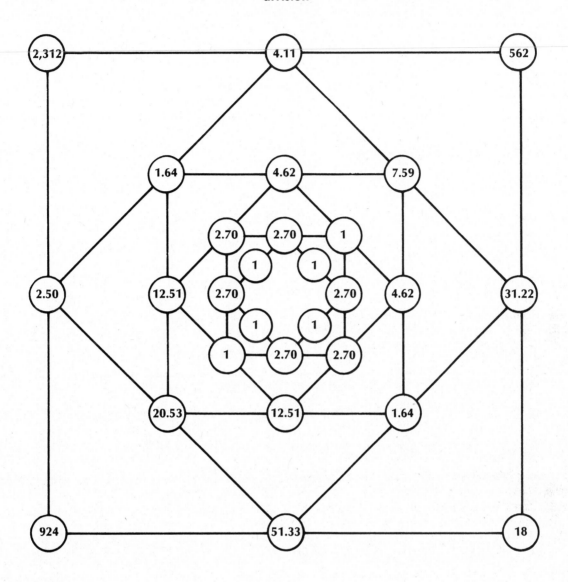

variations

A similar process can also be completed for subtraction (see Subtraction Squares).

CHAPTER VII

fRACTiONS

◉◉◉◉◉◉◉◉◉◉◉◉◉

Children come to school with some knowledge of fractions; they can most likely recognize halves and perhaps fourths and thirds. However, because they have been allowed to work with imperfect models, they often possess misconceived ideas about fractional numbers. To a young child, taking one-half a cookie may mean nothing more than not to take all of the cookie; he may, in fact, ask for the big half.

One of the first tasks to be dealt with is that of fractional congruence. That is, if a paper plate is cut into two halves, then each half must be physically the same as the other, etc. This concept should, in turn, be followed by a physical comparison of fractional values. As examples, one-half is greater than one-fourth, but two-fourths equal one-half, etc. When students understand these ideas in relation to both the concept of a fraction of one-whole and the concept of a fraction of a group, they will be ready to begin operations on fractions.

The first activity in this chapter, Paper Plate Fractions, will give students tactile experiences with fraction equivalence concepts. Then, Fraction Family Card Games denote methods for working with pictorial and abstract representations of fractional parts of groups as well as wholes.

Three of the included activities compare the value of selected fractions. The first is Fraction Roulette that makes use of spinners or dice and an element of chance. The second is Calculating and Comparing that calls for a chart of equivalent fractions, decimals, and percentages. Finally, Match a Fraction is a card game that requires students to match pictorial and abstract fractional representations.

◉◉◉◉◉◉◉◉◉◉◉◉◉◉◉◉◉◉◉◉◉◉◉◉◉◉◉

Operations on fractions are included in the three remaining activities. They are Fraction and Decimal Magic Squares, Fraction Multiplication and Division Diagrams, and Fraction Operation Factor Puzzles.

In addition to the activities described here, certain ones from other chapters in this book might also be adapted to help students learn fraction concepts. Some of these are Noisy Boxes and Box Puzzles from Chapter I, Math Jigsaw Puzzles and Subtraction Squares in Chapter IV, Math File Folders and Checkerboard Math from Chapter VIII, plus Practicing Basics with Hand-Held Calculators from Chapter X.

paper plate fractions

(grades 3–6)

purposes

To give students tactile experiences with fraction concepts

To develop fraction equivalence concepts

preparation

Purchase about 200 very lightweight paper plates (get varied colors if available) at a discount or grocery store. Each child will need six plates plus scissors and a crayon or marking pen. Also, make a spinner with sections for 1/2, 1/4, 1/8, 1/3, and 1/6.

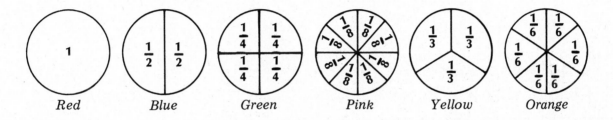

Red   Blue   Green   Pink   Yellow   Orange

directions

Instruct the students to take a red plate and mark it with a 1 for one whole amount. Then, have them draw a line through the center of the blue plate and use scissors to cut the plate apart along this line. Note that each part is one-half or one whole divided into two equal parts. Continue the process with each green plate being cut into one-fourths or one whole divided into four equal parts, each pink plate into one-eighths, etc.

Next, have the students practice finding how many 1/2s, 1/4s, etc., equal one whole. Also, how many 1/4s = 1/2, 1/8s = 1/4, etc. Note specifically that the 1/2, 1/4, and 1/8 pieces do mesh, and that the 1/3 and 1/6 do also, but that they will not be able to equate 1/3s and 1/4s, etc.

If the students have mastered the concepts noted above, they may be introduced to an activity called "Put Together One Whole." To play, the students will need their paper plate fractional cutouts and a spinner (see below). They will use their red or one whole paper plate as their individual gameboard and, with each spin of the spinner, they may choose whether or not they wish to lay the corresponding fractional part on top of the red plate. The object is to put together enough fractional pieces to equal exactly one whole. In the example noted below, the fractions spun so far were 1/4, 1/3, 1/8, 1/2 and 1/6. Player one opted not to use 1/3 or 1/6, and player two did not use 1/8 or 1/2. Thus, in order to equal exactly one whole, player one needs 1/8 and player two needs 1/4.

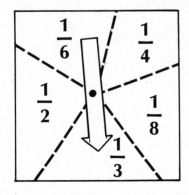
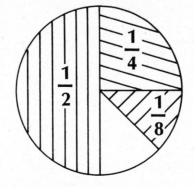
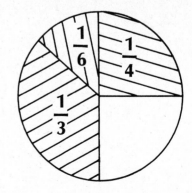

variations

The paper plate type of activity could be expanded to include other common fractions such as 1/9, 1/12, and 1/16. Work with decimal fractions including .1, .01, and .001 might also be utilized particularly as students study the metric system.

fraction family card games

(grades 3–6)

purposes

To give students pictorial experiences with fractional parts of wholes and fractional portions of groups

To reinforce concepts of fraction values

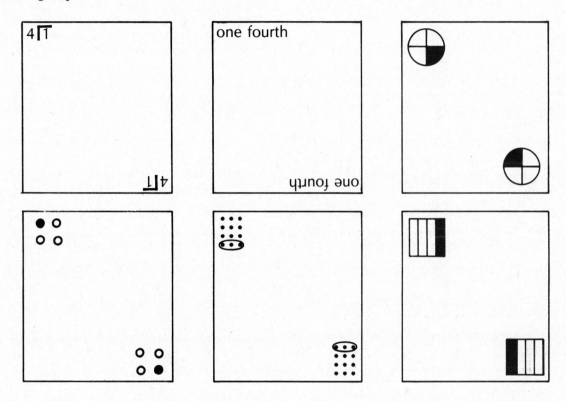

preparation

Obtain a deck of blank playing cards (or cut 3" X 5" index cards in half) and make a set of six cards to illustrate each of the commonly used fractions: 1/2, 1/3, 1/4, 1/6, 1/8, 1/10, 1/12, and 1/16 (sample above). Also prepare envelopes (or small boxes) with the corresponding fractions written on the outside of them.

directions

As soon as students are familiar with the various ways of representing each fraction, have them practice inserting the cards into the proper envelopes.

Once they are able to accomplish the card-sorting task without too much difficulty, explain how two to four of them might play a

Fraction Rummy card game. That is, the cards should be mixed and seven dealt to each player. The remaining cards are placed in a pile face down, and the top card is turned over and placed next to the pile. The players then check their cards and if they have any matching fraction pairs, they lay them on the table. The game proceeds with the player to one side of the dealer picking up either the turned-over card or the top one from the pile. If she obtains a matching card, she may lay the pair on the table, but whether she does or not, she must discard one card and place it face up beside the pile. Play continues in this manner until one player is rid of all her cards. The player with the most matching pairs is the winner.

Another game that can be played with the same cards is Fraction War. From two to six players may take part. The cards are mixed and seven are dealt face down to each of the players who put them in a pile without looking at them. The extra cards are set aside in a pile to be used later. At a signal every player turns over her top card, and the player with the largest (or smallest) fraction takes all of the turned-up cards. In the case of a tie, those players draw from the extra card pile, and the one obtaining the largest fractional amount gets the cards. The winner is the player who is able to take the greatest (or least) number of cards in a specified time.

variations

Playing the above games can be made more challenging by using mixed numbers, improper fractions, decimals, or even percentages.

fRACTioN RouleTTE

(grades 5–8)

purposes

To reinforce improper and mixed number fraction concepts

To compare the values of fractions reduced to lowest terms

preparation

Construct two spinners as shown below. The students will need pencil and paper. You may also want them to have available the Paper Plate Fractions that they constructed earlier.

Spinner 1

Spinner 2

directions

Fraction Roulette can be played in two different ways. The first way is to have a player spin both spinners and then use the two pointed numbers for the greatest (or least) fraction value. The spinners above point to 10 and 8; thus, the greatest fraction is 10/8 = 1 2/8 = 1 1/4. His opponent then spins both spinners again, and perhaps they point to 9 and 8; thus, the greatest value for this combination is 9/8 = 1 1/8. If both students agree that 1 1/4 is greater than 1 1/8, student one earns a point and the game continues in this manner. However, if they do not agree, the Paper Plate Fractions (constructed for an earlier activity) can be used in order to compare 1 1/4 and 1 1/8. Further questions, such as how much larger is 1 1/4, might be asked. This could require closer comparison or subtraction computation.

A second way to play Fraction Roulette involves having each student work with his own spinner and then compare results with an opponent. For example, if a boy used spinner 1 and the point of his spinner was at 7 while the feathered end was at 6, his fraction would be 7/6. A girl using spinner 2 might end with 5/4. Since the girl has the larger fraction, she can score a point by correctly finding the difference, or 5/4 – 7/6 = ___?___. The student with the most points after a prescribed number of spins is the winner.

calculating and comparing

(grades 5-8)

purposes

To compare equivalent fractions, decimals, and percentages through calculations and pictorial representations

To broaden a student's understanding of the related concepts for fractions, decimals, and percentages

preparation

Construct a large fraction, division, decimal, and percent comparison chart as shown. The backing might be of tagboard or simply a wall or table top, and the four columns can easily be made from adding machine paper tape that is glued or taped in place.

When the activity begins, the students will need a marking pen. It would also be very helpful, but not required, to have a hand-held calculator available.

directions

Together with the students, write the most commonly used fractions, from least to greatest, in the fraction column (some samples are shown above). Once this has been completed, discuss the fact that operations with fractions require division to take place and that any fraction could be expressed as a division problem. For example, ⅛ could be expressed as 8⟌1 . The next step, of course, is to have the students determine and list the division problems that are equivalent to the listed fractions.

Once the fractions have been set forth as division problems, the next step is to complete the division computation for each fraction in order to determine the decimal equivalent. For example, ⅛ = 8⟌1.000 = .125, which should be written in the decimal column. At this point, a hand-held calculator could speed up the computation process, especially for less able students, or it might be used to check results that had been determined by longhand division.

The percentage equivalent to the fraction being considered can now easily be determined by simply multiplying the decimal by 100. For example ⅛ = 8⟌1 = .125 and .125 × 100 = 12.5%. As soon as the 12.5% has been listed in

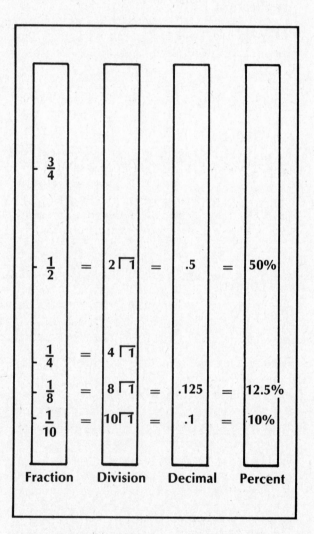

the proper row of the percent column, you can now review the alternate ways of recording ⅛ and perhaps discuss where in everyday life these forms of ⅛ are commonly used.

Once these calculations and comparisons have been completed for each fraction being considered, the students will likely emerge with a better understanding of fractions, decimals, and percentages.

96

MATCH A FRACTION

(grades 5–8)

purpose

To reinforce equivalent fraction, decimal, and percentage concepts

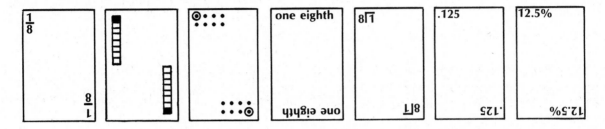

preparation

You will need a blank deck of playing cards (or cut 3" × 5" index cards in half) and a marking pen. Use the pen to mark equivalent fraction cards (see ⅛ illustrated above) for each of the fractions ⅛, ¼, ⅜, ½, ⅝, ¾, and ⅞.

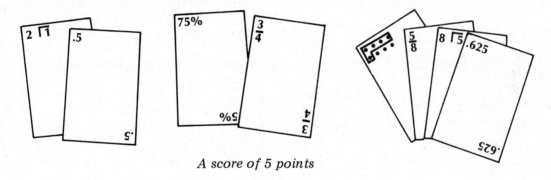

A score of 5 points

directions

Match a Fraction is a card game for two to four players. The dealer shuffles the cards and distributes seven to each player. She puts the remaining cards face down in a draw pile and turns up the top card.

Players check their cards and lay any matching pairs on the table in front of them. They score a point for each pair and an extra point for each additional card that matches the original pair.

The first player draws either the turned-up card or one from the draw pile. If she completes a pair, she lays it in front of her. In any case, she must also discard one card face up beside the draw pile. Play continues with each player taking turns until someone is able to lay down all of her cards.

Each player keeps a record of her points for each hand. The winner is the player with the most points after a specified time or number of hands.

variation

Match a Fraction could also be played at a more difficult level where fractions and operations on fractions must be considered. As an illustra-tion of one such situation, the following frac-tion cards do match.

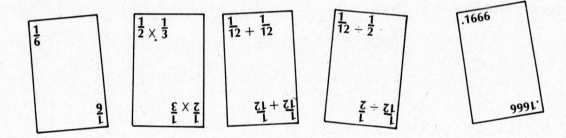

fraction and decimal magic squares

(grades 5–8)

purposes

To provide practice in adding common fractions and mixed numbers or decimals

To allow for the immediate checking of answers

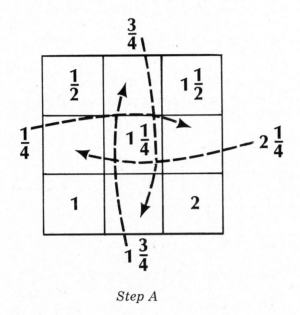

Step A

$\frac{1}{2}$	$1\frac{3}{4}$	$1\frac{1}{2}$
$2\frac{1}{4}$	$1\frac{1}{4}$	$\frac{1}{4}$
1	$\frac{3}{4}$	2

Magic square sum = $3\frac{3}{4}$

Step B

preparation

Draw a 3X3 grid and insert fractions (or decimals) as shown in Step A above. The inserted fractions should be in an evenly spaced sequence (as ¼, ½, ¾, 1, etc.) on the diagonal from left to right. Next, move the fractions that are displayed outside the grid as indicated by the arrows. The magic square grid will now appear as in Step B above.

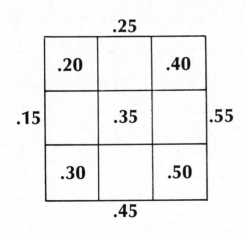

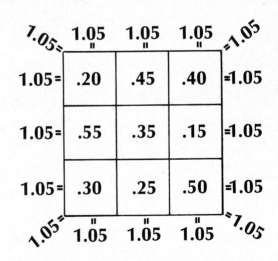

99

directions

Set forth a fraction magic square and have the students prove that it is, in fact, "magic" by adding in all directions (sixteen problems). If all fractional sums are the same, then their computation has been completed correctly.

Once the students become proficient at "proving" magic squares, then leave out one to four fractions and have them determine the missing ones. On a slightly more difficult level, you might insert one or two fractions that do not belong in the magic square and suggest that they determine any "wrong fractions" and insert the correct ones in their place.

variations

You may wish to help some of the students to learn to construct their own fraction magic squares. In fact, the more adept students may want to mix common fractions, whole numbers, mixed numbers, and decimal fractions as shown below. At this point, a hand-held calculator might be very helpful.

$\frac{1}{8}$	.4375	$\frac{3}{8}$
$\frac{9}{16}$	$\frac{5}{16}$	.0625
.25	$\frac{3}{16}$	$\frac{1}{2}$

Solution $= \frac{15}{16}$ or .9375

.6	2.6	$2\frac{1}{5}$
$3\frac{40}{100}$	1.8	.2
$1\frac{4}{10}$	1	3

Solution = 5.4 or $5\frac{4}{10}$

fraction multiplication and division diagrams

(grades 5–8)

purpose

To give students pictorial concepts of multiplication and division of fractions

preparation

Obtain a supply of graph paper and distribute two or three sheets to each student. Colored pencils may also be utilized. *See Appendix B, Item 8, for reproducible grid paper.

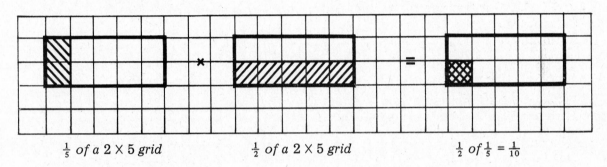

$\frac{1}{5}$ *of a 2 × 5 grid* $\frac{1}{2}$ *of a 2 × 5 grid* $\frac{1}{2}$ *of* $\frac{1}{5} = \frac{1}{10}$

$$\frac{1}{2} \times \frac{1}{5} = \underline{\quad}$$

directions

Use large graph paper or an overhead projector to work through several problems with your students. For example, with a problem such as 1/2 × 1/5 = _____ (illustrated above), begin by helping the students to see they will need to use a 2 × 5 grid as noted in the denominators of the two fractions. Then mark out 1/5 of the 2 × 5 grid and 1/2 of the same area and note that 1/2 of 1/5 equals 1 out of the 10 grid spaces. Thus,

1/2 × 1/5 = 1/10.

A similar process may be used when dividing a fraction by a fraction. For example, ¼ ÷ ⅓ = _____ (illustrated below) requires the use of a grid area that is 4 spaces by 3 spaces. As such, ¼ of the grid requires the marking out of 3 squares and ⅓ of the next grid has 4 squares denoted. Thus, ¼ ÷ ⅓ is illustrated as 3 squares divided by 4 squares resulting in ¾.

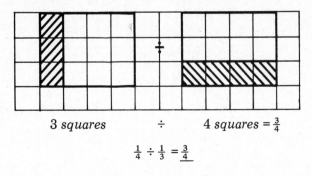

3 squares ÷ *4 squares* = $\frac{3}{4}$

$$\frac{1}{4} \div \frac{1}{3} = \frac{3}{4}$$

variations

Mixed numbers can also be dealt with in this manner. The problem $1\frac{1}{3} \times 2\frac{1}{4} = $ _____ could be dealt with as:

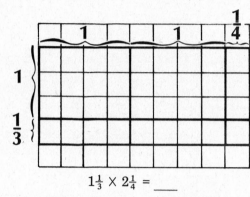

(Note: 1 whole area is 3 × 4 or 12 spaces)

$$1\frac{1}{3} \times 2\frac{1}{4} = \underline{}$$

$$\frac{4}{3} \times \frac{9}{4} = \frac{36}{12} \text{ or } 3 \text{ (whole areas)}$$

However, the same numerals used in a division format yield quite a different result. Thus, $1\frac{1}{3} \div 2\frac{1}{4} = $ _____ may be illustrated as:

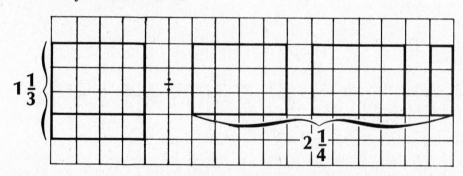

$$(16 \text{ squares}) \div (27 \text{ squares}) = \frac{16}{27}$$

or

$$1\frac{1}{3} \quad \div \quad 2\frac{1}{4} \quad =$$

$$\frac{4}{3} \quad \div \quad \frac{9}{4} \quad =$$

$$\frac{4}{3} \quad \times \quad \frac{4}{9} \quad = \frac{16}{27}$$

fraction operation factor puzzles

(grades 5–8)

purposes

To provide practice in adding, subtracting, multiplying, or dividing fractions

To allow for the immediate checking of results

preparation

Using a pen and ruler, mark a piece of tagboard into 1" squares (illustrated below is a 5×5 factor puzzle). Next, write fraction operation problems and the corresponding answers in alternate squares. You may also wish to insert random fractions into the outside positions where no answers would be placed (noted >). Cut out the puzzle pieces in random fashion (the greater the number of pieces, the more difficult the puzzle becomes) and put the pieces into an envelope.

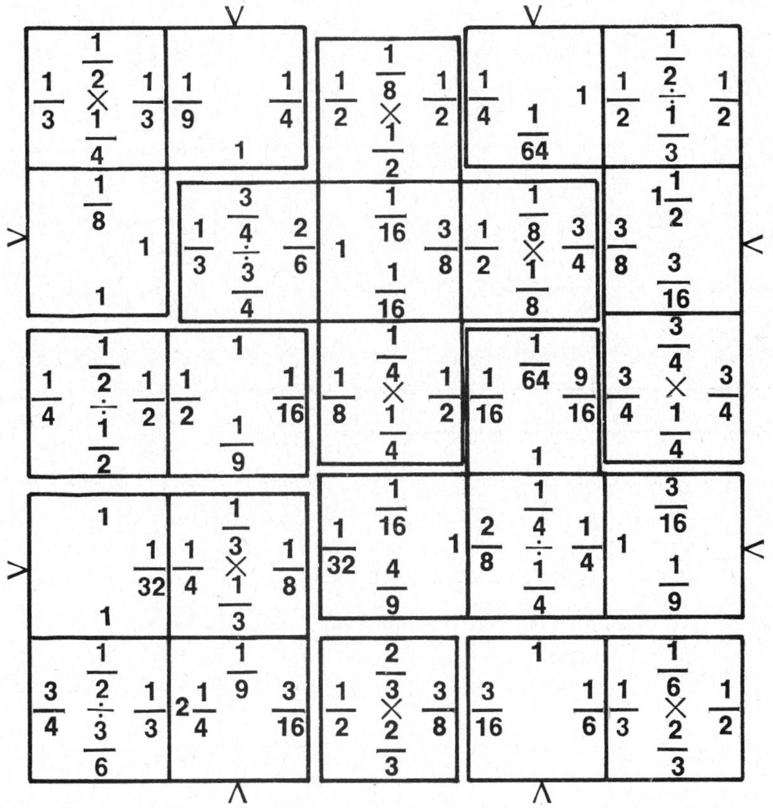

directions

Each student using a Fraction Operation Factor Puzzle should be instructed to take the pieces out of the envelope and mix them thoroughly. He should then match the factors and answers in such a manner that they are aligned vertically and horizontally. The completed factor puzzle will be a rectangle similar to the one shown above.

103

CHAPTER VIII

MULTIPURPOSE AIDS AND ACTIVITIES

◉◉◉◉◉◉◉◉◉◉◉◉

One teacher may wish to select an activity or game that can be used to help students learn or practice a variety of mathematical concepts. On the other hand, another teacher may wish to prescribe several activities that teach or reinforce the same concept. The games, aids, and activities in this chapter can all be utilized in a number of ways; thus, the teacher may select mathematical activities appropriate for her students.

Several of the activities may be played with scrap materials or preexisting gameboards and a minimum of preparation. These are Balance It, Scramble, and Checkerboard Math. Others may be assembled with materials from the school supply room or your kitchen cupboards. In this category are Shuffleboard Mathematics, Math File Folders, Tinfoil Math Boards, Chalkboard Spinner Games, and Equation Bingo. The rest—Number Grid, Capture a Numeral, TV Show Math, and Operation 500 —are easily reproduced with dittoed copies.

Some of the games, aids, and activities from other chapters in this book may also be modified for multiple uses. Included are Math Ball and Box Puzzles from Chapter I, Math Jigsaw Puzzles and Punch-Out Figures in Chapter IV, Multiplication Grid Diagrams and Hookey in Chapter V, plus Practicing Basics with Hand-Held Calculators from Chapter X.

◉◉◉◉◉◉◉◉◉◉◉◉◉◉◉◉◉◉◉◉◉◉◉◉◉◉

bAlance it

(grades k–8)

purposes

To provide practice in counting, addition, subtraction, multiplication, or division

To improve fine motor control while also allowing an element of chance

preparation

Secure fifteen to thirty miscellaneous shaped wooden blocks. Small leftover pieces can usually be obtained free from a cabinet shop or from a site where a new building is being constructed.

Use a marking pen to write a numeral (or a number of dots) on one surface of each block.

directions

Balance It can be played by two or more players. The teacher should indicate whether the game is to be played by counting, addition, subtraction, division, or any combination thereof, and then place the starting block on the playing surface. For example, when playing Addition Balance It (see illustration), student A places the number 7 block on top of the 5 block, and if he can compute $5 + 7 = 12$, he begins with 12 points.

Student B then tries to score $5 + 7 + 3 = 15$. The game continues in this manner with additional points being obtained each time a student balances and correctly computes a new addition sum.

However, if a student fails to balance a block or if his computation has not been correct, then his opponent can obtain those points by correctly computing that addition sum. The winner is the student who has obtained the greatest total score up to the time when the blocks fall.

Counting Balance It might be played by lower-grade students with blocks that have dots on them. Each time a student is able to balance a block and count the number of dots on it, he would receive a point. When the Balance It blocks fall, the student with the most points is the winner.

Advanced students might play a game of

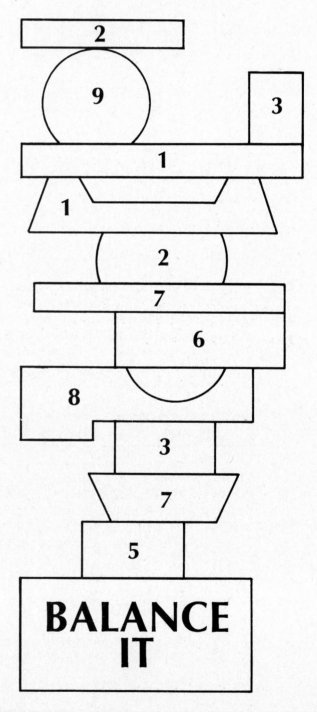

Combination Balance It where any operation can be used to try and obtain a selected answer. For example, with 500 as the target answer (the underlined numbers are from the illustration above) the game might proceed as: $\underline{5} \times \underline{7} = 35$, $35 \times \underline{3} = 105$, $105 - \underline{8} = 97$, $97 \times \underline{6} = 582$, $582 - \underline{7} = 575$, $575 \div \underline{2} = 287.5$. $287.5 - \underline{1} = 286.5$, $286.5 \times \underline{1} = 286.5$. $286.5 \div \underline{3} = 95.5$, $95.5 \times \underline{9} = 859.5$, $859.5 \div \underline{2} = 429.75$.

variations

At times students may not wish to keep score, but simply enjoy seeing who can put the last block on the pile. Balance It might also be played with operations on common or decimal fractions.

shuffleboard MATHEMATICS
(grades k–8)

purpose

To give practice with numeral identification or addition, subtraction, multiplication, and division computation

preparation

Prepare a shuffleboard surface (see illustration) on a tabletop, floor, playground, etc. Also, obtain nine bean bags, wooden discs, or plastic coffee can lids and use a marking pen to write the numerals 1–9 on them.

directions

Shuffleboard Mathematics is usually played by two students. One player stands at each end of the shuffleboard, and the teacher designates the numbered discs and the mathematical operations that are to be worked with. For example, Student A is asked to slide discs 4, 5, and 6 toward the opposite end of the shuffleboard and add the disc numbers to the shuffleboard numbers that they touched. After doing so, her disc locations (see illustration) require her to add $4 + 1 = 5, 5 + 7 = 12$ and $6 + 4 + 5 + 8 + 9 = 32$. Her cumulative total is then $5 + 12 + 32 = 49$. Her opponent then uses the same discs to try and achieve a greater sum. However, if one of the students makes a computation error and this is corrected by her opponent, the opponent then receives the score for that particular disc and she adds it to her own cumulative total. The game continues in this manner until one of the students has achieved a designated score or until each has taken a specific number of turns.

Students working at an earlier stage of mathematics might simply name the numeral that their discs landed on and show (with fingers or concrete objects) the "how manyness" of that numeral. On the other hand, students at upper-grade levels might use any combination of operations to try and achieve a specific answer. For example, using the same illustrated numbers, if 210 was the target answer, then $\{(4 + 1) \cdot (5 + 7) \cdot (4)\} - (6 + 5 + 8 + 9) = 212$ would come quite close.

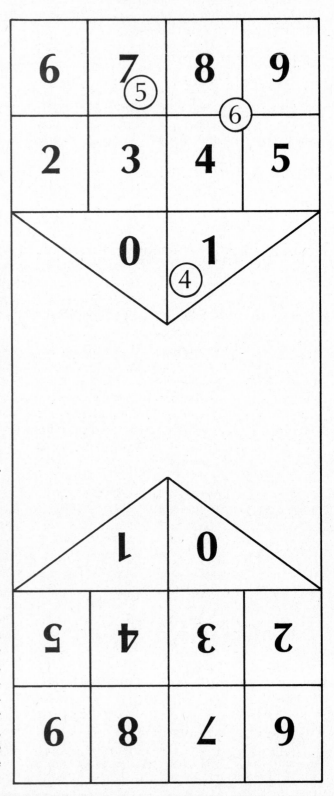

MATH fILE fOLDERS

(grades k–8)

purposes

To provide practice with basic facts, computation, story problems, etc.

To encourage individualized work and self-checking of answers

To provide an alternate means for testing students.

preparation

You will need a supply of manila file folders, library pocket envelopes, glue, 3" × 5" index cards, and marking pens.

On the inside of the folders, glue the library pockets as needed for the operation (sample folders are shown). Then take the marking pens and write appropriate problems and answers on the index cards and the library pockets. If the folders are to be utilized for testing situations, you may want to mark some of the index cards so that they do not match any library pocket in the file folder. You will want to make a series of Math File Folders to use as students need additional work in selected mathematical areas. Thus, one teacher may make use of a series of folders having to do with telling time, another with division facts, etc.

directions

When a student needs supplemental work with a specific mathematical concept, the teacher may take a related Math File Folder from his cabinet and ask the student to put all of the answer cards into the matching pockets. If pencil and paper computation is necessary, the student can do this on small pieces of scratch paper and put these into the same pocket as the answer card. The teacher can then check the student's work, or the student can check his own work if the corresponding answer or problem has been written on the back of the card (or if a separate answer key is kept in the answer pocket).

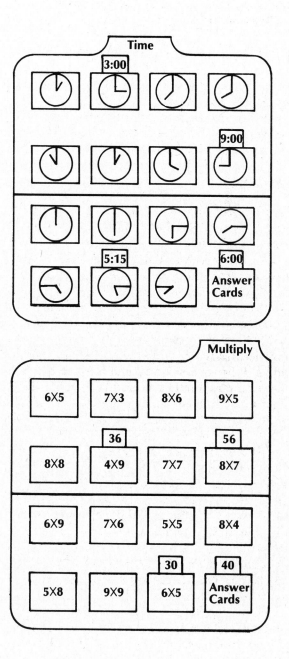

variations

In some situations work tasks might be set forth that require the use of small equipment items that are stored in the Math File Folder. For example, students might be asked to find the length and width of the classroom, a table top, a student desk top, and so on, to the closest centimetre. To accomplish this, a metre tape would be provided in the folder together with instructions, etc.

Another variation would be to use a kind of self-correcting key punch card in the file folder (see illustration below). To construct this type of folder an assortment of colors is used on an answer checking grid, and 3" X 5" index cards are punched so that the correct answer color

will only be displayed through one hole when aligned with the checking grid. The problems on the index cards are written in the same color ink that will show through the proper answer hole. For example, the problem $5 + 7 = \triangle$ (see below) has the possible answers 11, 12, and 57 punched out, but since the problem is written in green ink, the answer will show through in green. Since 57 shows red and 11 shows blue, they cannot be correct; but the hole next to 12 shows green, therefore indicating that it is the correct answer. This self-correcting procedure may be used with any computation problem, story problems, matching geometric figures and names, etc.

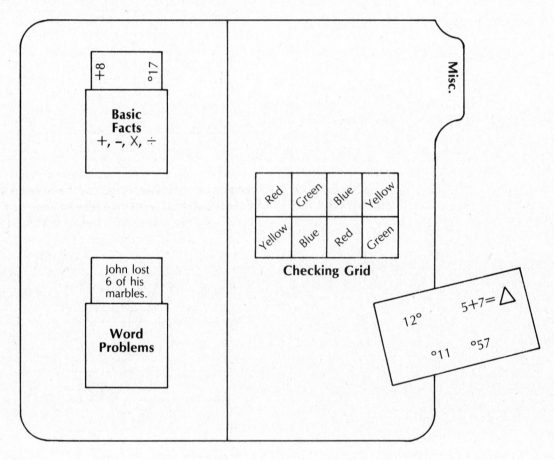

Checking Grid

110

tinfoil math boards

(grades k–8)

purpose

To provide a means of instantly comparing basic facts and answers, computations and results, etc.

preparation

You will need tinfoil (aluminum kitchen foil), masking tape, tagboard, marking pens, and a paper punch to construct Tinfoil Math Boards. Also necessary will be insulated electric wire, a flashlight bulb and receptacle, a flashlight battery, small wood board to hold these items (see C below), and a soldering gun plus solder. (Note: if you do not wish to construct this wired lighting device, you may purchase similar ones at stores such as Radio Shack.)

The Tinfoil Math Board is constructed by first writing mathematical problems and the corresponding answers on the playing surface. Then, next to each problem and answer, a hole is punched (see A below). Now, turn the board over and lay a narrow strip of tinfoil (approximately ¼" wide) from the punched hole at the problem to the corresponding one at the answer, and cover it with masking tape (see B below), which both holds it in place and serves as insulation. Repeat the process between each problem and answer until all have been completed. You will want to make a series of these boards at levels appropriate for your students.

The lighting device can be constructed (see C below) by fastening the battery and the light receptacle to the board with tape or strong rubber bands. Then solder the wires to the battery (also to the bulb if no receptacle is available) as shown.

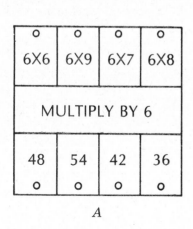

A

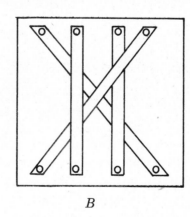

B

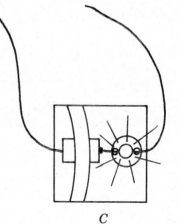

C

directions

Check the lighting device by touching the ends of the two wires together and, if the bulb lights, everything is ready to go. Then, select a Tinfoil Math Board and tell the student that if she touches the proper combinations with the ends of her wires, the bulb will light up. However, she should first write the problem and what she thinks is the answer on her own paper, and then she should check it on the Tinfoil Math Board. For example, if she had written $6 \times 9 = 54$ and checked it on the board, the light would come on. However, a check of $6 \times 8 = 42$ would prove to be incorrect and the light would not function.

chalkboard spinner games

(grades k–8)

purposes

To provide skill practice for most number and operation concepts

To allow an element of chance

preparation

You will need a suction cup, a short bolt, a piece of heavy poster board, and a large paper clip. The poster board should be cut into the shape of an arrow approximately 3" X 18", and a small hole should be punched through it at the central balancing point. Now insert the short bolt through the hole and attach it to the suction cup (see illustration below). A suction cup of this type—from ¾" to 1 ½" in diameter—may be purchased in most hardware stores or obtained from a child's dart gun set. Finally, suction the arrow to the chalkboard and spin it several times to see if it is balanced. If it is not, then attach the large paper clip as shown and slide it back and forth along the arrow until balance is achieved.

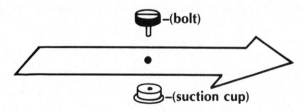

directions

Attach the arrow to the chalkboard with the suction cup and write numerals in a circle around it. Next, provide the format for a mathematical problem but do not put any numbers on it. For example, if place value is of concern, the students might be asked to put four blanks on their papers as ⎯, ⎯ ⎯ ⎯ into which they will insert a number with each spin of the spinner. Further, once a number has been written—and you must write each number immediately after each spin—it may not be moved. The work of three students is shown here:

$\underline{7},\underline{8}\,\underline{9}\,\underline{3}$	$\underline{8},\underline{7}\,\underline{3}\,\underline{9}$	$\underline{9},\underline{7}\,\underline{8}\,\underline{3}$
Student A	*Student B*	*Student C*

The numbers spun in order were 7, 3, 8, and 9. Thus, Student C is the winner because he achieved the numeral with the greatest place value.

In another situation the students might be playing a subtraction game where a two-digit number is to be subtracted from a three-digit number for the smallest remainder. As such their work might appear as:

1 2 9	2 6 1	2 1 8
− 8 6	− 8 9	− 6 9
4 3	1 7 2	1 4 9
Student A	*Student B*	*Student C*

Thus, when the numbers 6, 8, 2, 9, and 1 were spun, Student A became the winner since his remainder was the smallest.

variations

Chalkboard Spinner Games can be modified to fit many formats. Young children, for instance, might simply be asked to name the numeral that the spinner is pointing to and to show with objects how many that numeral represents.

More advanced students might play spinner games relating to division or decimal fractions. Such activities can further be used with the whole class, small groups, or as learning-center activities.

SCRAMBLE

(grades 2–8)

purposes

To reinforce basic addition, subtraction, multiplication, and division facts

To practice rapid mental or pencil and paper computation

preparation

You will need different colored marking pens and 20, 30, or 40 index cards (3" × 5") depending on the number of students in your class. Each set of ten cards should be marked with the numerals 0–9 in a particular color. Thus, for a class of twenty-eight students it would be necessary to have ten cards with the numerals 0–9 in red, ten in blue, and ten in green.

Red team = winner

Green team = wrong order

directions

Pass out the colored numeral cards, one to each student. (If there are not quite enough students for full teams of ten, a few students may need to hold two cards.) Each student's team is determined by the color of the numeral she is holding—such as the red, green, or blue team. Tell the students that they are to Scramble (run or walk) to the answer location for their team if their particular numeral is part of the required answer. That is, for example, if 8 + 9 is called

by the teacher, the 1 and the 7 card holders from each team will try to get to their answer location and display their cards in the proper order before the members of the other teams reach their locations. The team members to do so first score a point for their team. In case of a tie, a rematch can be called by the teacher or duplicate points can be awarded. The team with the highest score wins.

115

Any basic fact problem or one requiring computation might be called out by the teacher.

Some possible problems and the card solutions are displayed below:

(1) 3 plus 4 = $\boxed{7}$

(2) 17 minus 5 = $\boxed{1}\,\boxed{2}$

(3) 9 times 8 = $\boxed{7}\,\boxed{2}$

(4) 72 divided by 9 = $\boxed{8}$

(5) The remainder to 108 divided by 12 = $\boxed{0}$

(6) 34 times 52 = $\boxed{1}\,\boxed{7}\,\boxed{6}\,\boxed{8}$

(7) The common fraction for .75 = $\dfrac{\boxed{3}}{\boxed{4}}$

NUMbER GRid

(grades 3–8)

purposes

To give practice with basic addition, subtraction, multiplication, and division facts

To challenge advanced students to locate equations which utilize more than one operation

preparation

Prepare duplicate copies of a Number Grid similar to the one shown below. As the grid is prepared, be certain that several possible equation combinations (for the operations that the students need to practice) are included.

```
 9      6     81     42      7      6     19

45      2     27      8      6      8     25
              =
 5      7      3      5      1     14      7
              X
21      4      9      6     14      3     11
  =
56      7     28      2     15      2      9
    X                              X
 3     18      2      3     10      8      3
                                          X
36      9     14      2     28     42  =   7
```

*See Appendix B, Item 13, for a reproducible Number Grid.

directions

Instruct the students to find equations in the Number Grid. Explain to them that each equation must use adjacent numbers and that they should include all operations signs, grouping symbols, and equal signs before a loop is drawn around it. You might restrict them to one operation, perhaps multiplication, and see who can find the most correct equations.

In another instance the student who is able to come up with the longest equation might be the winner. Thus, it is up to the teacher to designate the most meaningful experiences.

EQUATION bingo

(grades 3–8)

purpose

To provide practice with basic addition, subtraction, multiplication, and division facts and computations

preparation

Prepare a blank Equation Bingo card for each student (on tagboard or on dittoed copies). Then, as a series of number facts or computations are discussed and practiced, have the students record each at random positions on their own cards. Also, mark one of the positions "Free" and provide each player with a number of markers (plastic discs, corn, etc.). In addition, the teacher needs to prepare a "caller's card" (the answer) for each equation as well as a few caller's cards that do not match any equation practiced.

A 3 × 3 bingo card

3+3	6+3	15–9
10–7	Free	13–11
4+6	9–5	7+8

6

Caller's cards

directions

The teacher mixes the caller's cards and places them in a pile face down. The top card is turned over; for example, 6. At this point if a student thinks he has an equation on his board that matches the answer called out, he may cover it with a marker. Play continues in this manner until some player has a complete row covered horizontally, vertically, or diagonally. Then, before he can be designated the winner, the player must call out each equation in the line and its correct answer. Of course, the teacher must also check the caller's cards to be certain that each answer has been given.

variations

Equation Bingo could also be played on a 5 × 5 board in standard bingo form where the column is designated by a letter. For example, B-3 would mean that the player must have an equation with an answer of 3 under the B column. Thus, another pile of cards with letters B-I-N-G-O (repeated several times) would need to be turned over at the same time as the caller's cards in order to complete Equation Bingo in this manner.

cHeckerboard MatH

(grades 4–8)

purposes

To provide practice with basic arithmetic facts

To supplement computation skill practice

preparation

You will need a checkboard and checkers, masking tape, and a marking pen. Tear off fifteen or more short pieces of masking tape, write basic fact problems on them (or computation problems), and stick them randomly on the playing squares of the checkerboard.

directions

Checkerboard Math is played with exactly the same rules as the standard checker game with one exception. The one difference is that a player cannot jump or move to a square having a problem on it unless she can answer the problem correctly.

variations

If large computation problems (such as 316 × 582) are utilized, their answers may be checked by use of an answer key or with a hand-held calculator.

CAPTURE A NUMERAL

(grades 5–8)

purposes

To provide practice with addition, subtraction, multiplication, and division

To develop logical thinking skills

preparation

Prepare a ditto master with the numerals 1–100 (as shown below) and duplicate enough copies for all players. Also, mark a deck of forty blank playing cards (or 3" X 5" index cards cut in half) with five cards each for the numerals 2–9.

1	2	3	4	5	6	7	8	9	10
11	12	13	14	15	16	17	18	19	20
21	22	23	24	25	26	27	28	29	30
31	32	33	34	35	36	37	38	39	40
41	42	43	44	45	46	47	48	49	50
51	52	53	54	55	56	57	58	59	60
61	62	63	64	65	66	67	68	69	70
71	72	73	74	75	76	77	78	79	80
81	82	83	84	85	86	87	88	89	90
91	92	93	94	95	96	97	98	99	100

*See Appendix B, Item 14, for an enlarged copy of this Capture A Numeral gameboard.

directions

Capture a Numeral may be played by two to four players at a time. One player begins by mixing the cards and dealing 5 to each player. Player number one then attempts to Capture a Numeral from the board by declaring one or more operations on two or more of his cards. He places the cards in front of him and states his problem: for example, $(7 \times 9) + 8 = 71$. If everyone agrees he is correct, his name is written across the numeral on everyone's playing sheet. However, if there is a dispute, it is settled by completing the operation on a hand-held calculator. If the player is not correct, he loses his turn and must keep the same cards, but if he did calculate correctly, those three cards are then placed in the discard pile and three new cards are taken from the face-down stack. Player two now tries to capture a different numeral in the same manner. The game continues in this fashion until one player has captured twenty numerals or until time is up.

TV SHOW MATH

(grades 5–8)

purposes

To provide addition, subtraction, multiplication, and division computation practice

To improve logical thinking abilities

preparation

Secure a current television schedule and note any programs which have numerals or number names in their titles, such as "Sixty Minutes" or "The Six Million Dollar Man." Then, devise

mathematical computation problems appropriate for your students that will yield those numbers and list them on a problem sheet as shown below.

---

(1) $2500 \div 50 =$ ___50___   _____ Hawaii Five-0 _____

(2) $(1000 - 995) \times (36 \div 3) =$ _____   _____

(3) $1000 + 459 + 333 + 207 =$ _____   _____

(4) $(4 + 1 - 3) \times 6 =$ _____   _____

(5) $6,000 \times 1,000 =$ _____   _____

Answers: (1) Hawaii Five-0, (2) Sixty Minutes, (3) Space 1999, (4) Adam 12, (5) Six Million Dollar Man

---

directions

Tell the students that each computation problem will yield a number from the title of a TV program. You may want to work a problem or two with them as they begin, such as $2500 \div 50$

$= 50$, where the answer is a part of the TV program title for "Hawaii Five-O." Then, see if they are able to find the other titles correctly.

variation

If students become very adept at this type of mathematical logic, give them a TV title number and have them devise their own problems.

See if they can determine two or three problems that will yield the same answer.

OPERATION 500

(grades 5-8)

purposes

To practice addition, subtraction, multiplication, and division computation

To improve logical thinking

preparation

Prepare an Operation 500 lap chart similar to the one shown below. The numbers for each lap may be of any size.

Lap 1	5	12	13	8	1		
Lap 2	11	8	7	6	4		
Lap 3	60	4	56	2	30		
Lap 4	7	6	1	3	7		
Lap 5	64	23	0	17	3		
Lap 6	1	7	8	4	6		
Lap 7	20	14	6	5	5		
Lap 8	21	25	0	3	2		

*See Appendix B, Item 15, for a reproducible Operation 500 worksheet.

TOTAL

directions

Instruct the students to write equations for each lap so that the total score from all eight laps will equal 500 or as close to it as possible. The order of the numbers within each lap, however, may be rearranged. Thus, one logical approach would be to have the score for each lap equal approximately 60. As such, lap 1 might appear as $(5 \times 12) + (13 - 8 - 1) = 64$ or $[(5 - 1) \times 13] + (12 - 8) = 56$. When a student's work is completed, it may be checked with a hand-held calculator. Any student who scores exactly 500 is a winner. However, if no student has 500, the student nearest that answer is the winner.

122

CHAPTER IX

pROblEM solvinG

◉◉◉◉◉◉◉◉◉◉

Very likely the most important facet of mathematics education today is problem solving. We cannot be certain what problems our students will have to solve in the future, but we do know that they will need to solve problems of many types. Thus, much of what we do in mathematics classes should be aimed at helping students to master a variety of techniques for problem solving.

Students will learn best how to solve word problems by solving many problems that require varied solution techniques. Three sections of the chapter—Problem-Solving Techniques, A Strategy for Analyzing Word Problems, and Other Aids for Problem Solving—note possible solution patterns. Then, a series of Oral Problems for Grades 1–6 are set forth as a technique to cause students to focus quickly on the important information in problems. Furthermore, since reading difficulties are directly related to many solution errors, one section titled Reading Word Problems suggests certain techniques for aiding students. Three sections—Simulated Problems, Student-Devised Problems, and Mathematics Problem Solving in Everyday Life—then deal with mathematical problem solving in daily life settings. Finally, because students enjoy them as a diversion, a section on Problem Puzzlers completes the chapter.

Certain activities from other chapters in this book might also be utilized for mathematical problem solving. Included could be Box Puzzles in Chapter I, Find a Million from Chapter II, Averaging Activities in Chapter VI, Math File Folders and TV Show Math from Chapter VIII, Problem Solving with Calculators and Hand-Held Calculators in the Grocery Store in Chapter X, plus several measurement activities from Chapter XI.

◉◉◉◉◉◉◉◉◉◉◉◉◉◉◉◉◉◉◉◉◉◉◉◉◉

pRoblEM–SOLVINg TECHNiQUES
(grades k–8)

purposes

To help students become successful in solving mathematical word problems

To enhance students' abilities to deal more successfully with everyday applied problem-solving situations

preparation and directions

As a teacher, there are a number of techniques you may utilize to help students become more proficient at solving word problems and to deal with applied mathematical situations. Some of the more pertinent suggestions, together with brief comments relating to them, are noted here:

1. *Present many varied word problems.*

   Students will show improvement in their ability to solve word problems if they simply have to solve many problems, but they will show even greater gains if systematic instruction to develop understanding is also provided by the teacher.

2. *Present problems orally.*

   Beginning with the kindergarten program, problems should be presented verbally. This procedure requires the student to "analyze" the important information in the problem quickly. It is also the manner in which many (perhaps most) out-of-school problem situations occur. Thus, a section titled Oral Problems for Grades 1–6 is presented later in this chapter.

3. *Teach reading of mathematics.*

   Teaching vocabulary and reading skills directly related to mathematics will improve student achievement with word problems. In brief, a student must be able to: (a) read the words and symbols, (b) attach literal meanings, (c) analyze relationships, (d) set up the related math equation, (e) compute, and (f) interpret the answer. A more complete look at these problem-

solving skills is presented in a later section of this chapter titled Reading Word Problems.

4. *Tape record problems.*

   Tape recordings of textbook exercises and other problems can often help students who have reading difficulties.

5. *Provide alternate techniques.*

   Word problems and applied mathematical situations are often solved in varying formats. Informal as well as formal methods often prove helpful to students. Some related considerations are: (a) getting the student "started" with the problem, (b) analyzing the information with various techniques, (c) making reasonable estimates, (d) setting up formulas, and (e) learning when tables, graphs, or pattern drawings can be of help. Further information relating to these items is presented in later sections of this chapter titled A Strategy for Analyzing Word Problems and Other Aids for Problem Solving.

6. *Have students work together.*

   Arrange for two or three students to work together as they analyze the information and write the related mathematical sentences. In doing so, they will take more time, but they will also solve more problems correctly.

7. *Help students check and verify their work.*

   The teacher should take time to discuss

any problem-solving errors with students. Verifying the way in which correct answers relate to the original problem is also very important.

8. *Ask "real life" problems.*

With the help of students, write problems that they are truly concerned about. For instance, a fifth-grade student may find a problem about space travel much more meaningful than another about a marble game. Also, when writing such problems, list the question first (rather than at the end of the problem as is usually found in textbooks); with problems encountered in everyday life, the problem is almost always given first.

9. *Require pupils to devise their own problems.*

Have the students share problems of concern from everyday life. Then build mathematical word problems from these areas of concern. Teachers of young children should write these problems in the children's own words. Older students, with some assistance, can write their own problems. Once a collection of such problems is available, each student should attempt to solve problems devised by other students; and, if difficulties are encountered, she can discuss the problem with the student who wrote it. A more complete description of this process is given in the section of this chapter titled Student-Devised Problems.

10. *Investigate how non-mathematicians solve applied mathematics problems.*

Find out how the homemaker, mechanic, farmer, carpenter, and other people solve mathematics problems in everyday life. For example, when a homemaker is making ½ a recipe and ¼ cup salad oil is called for, how does she figure it out? In school we would proceed $\frac{1}{2} \times \frac{1}{4} = \frac{1}{8}$, but at home she likely sights the level of the salad oil as she pours until it appears half way to the ¼ cup mark. In most instances out of the classroom, mental arithmetic and "short-cut" mathematics are used rather than pencil and paper problem solving. A more detailed look at this realm is provided later in this chapter in the section titled Mathematics Problem Solving in Everyday Life.

ORAl pRoblems foR GRAdes 1-6

(grades 1-6)

purposes

To cause students to "analyze" the important problem information quickly

To become more proficient in solving problems as they are generally dealt with in out-of-school settings

preparation

You will want to secure or devise a series of verbal problems that are appropriate for the students at your particular grade level. A list-ing of possible problems for grades 1 and 2, 3 and 4, and 5 and 6 follows.

directions and problems for grades 1 and 2

A. This is an exercise in listening as well as in working with numbers.
B. I will read to you five questions.
C. No grades will be taken on these questions. You will check your own answers.
D. These are nonpaper and nonpencil questions; that is, you listen to the question, think of the answer, and write the answer only on your paper.
E. Number your paper from one to five.

1. Karen has 2 dolls. Cheryl has 1 more doll than Karen has. How many dolls does Cheryl have? (3 dolls)
2. David has 4 toy cars. Michael has 3 toy cars. How many toy cars do both boys have? (7 cars)
3. John has 5 pieces of gum. Steven has 6 pieces of gum. Which boy has the most pieces of gum? (Steven)
4. Nancy is 43 inches tall. Susan is 40 inches tall. Which one is taller? (Nancy)
5. Larry went to the store and bought 5 apples. On the way home Jim gave Larry 1 apple. How many apples did Larry have when he got home? (6 apples)

6. Mary has 5 crayons in her box. Later the teacher gave her a yellow, an orange, and a purple crayon. How many crayons does she have now? (8 crayons)
7. John was asked to sharpen 10 pencils. Bill was asked to sharpen 6 pencils. Which boy has to sharpen more pencils? (John)
8. Ann has 3 cookies. Her mother gave her 2 more cookies. How many cookies does Ann have? (5 cookies)
9. Mark has a stick that is 7 inches long. Jim has a stick that is 9 inches long. Which boy has the longer stick? (Jim)
10. Sally brought 4 dolls to the tea party, and Jane brought 3 dolls. How many dolls did they have at the party? (7 dolls)

11. Tom had 25 marbles, and he gave 10 to his brother. How many did Tom have left? (15 marbles)
12. Mrs. Jones needs 100 napkins. If she already has 70, how many more does she need? (30 napkins)
13. Mary has 2 birds and 11 fish. How many pets does she have? (13 pets)
14. There are 20 students in our class. If ½ of them are absent, how many are present? (10 students)
15. Spark can bark 10 times without stopping. Larky can bark 8 times without stopping. How many more times can Spark bark than Larky can bark without stopping? (2 more barks)
16. If Ann brings 20 cookies and Kathy brings

10 cookies, how many cookies will they be bringing together? (30 cookies)

17. Joe has 2 pieces of cake and Bob has 4 pieces of cake. How many pieces do they have altogether? (6 pieces of cake)

18. Jack had 11 marbles and gave 3 to his little brother. How many marbles does Jack have left? (8 marbles)

19. Linda has 5 dolls and Mary has 6 dolls. How many dolls do they have altogether? (11 dolls)

20. Ken had 2 marbles. He won 5 more and then lost 3. How many marbles did he end up with? (4 marbles)

21. Sally's mother baked 12 cupcakes. Sally and her friends ate 7 of them. How many cupcakes are left? (5 cupcakes)

22. Paul wants to buy a pencil that costs 15¢. He has 8¢. How much more money does Paul need? (7¢)

23. Karen has 3 pieces of candy, Sue has 2 pieces of candy, and John has 5 pieces of candy. How many pieces of candy do they have altogether? (10 pieces of candy)

24. George has 2 dimes, 3 nickels, and 1 penny in his pocket. How much money does he have? (36¢)

25. Sam has 2 dogs, 3 goldfish, and 1 cat. How many animals does he have? (6 animals)

26. Mike threw the ball 9 feet and Ken threw the ball 14 feet. How much farther did Ken throw the ball than Mike? (5 feet)

27. Bill made 12 model airplanes. He gave 3 to John. How many did Bill have left? (9 model airplanes)

28. Sue put 12 balloons into groups of 4 each. How many groups of balloons did Sue have? (3 groups)

29. Jim bought one hot dog which cost 25¢. He paid the man with a one dollar bill. How much change did Jim get back? (75¢)

30. Tom had 12 red cars and 8 blue cars. How many more red cars than blue cars did Tom have? (4 more red cars)

31. It is 8:00 A.M. and Tom must be at school in 25 minutes. At what time will Tom have to be at school? (8:25 A.M.)

32. Mrs. Smith had 5 bowls, 4 plates, and 4 saucers. How many dishes did she have in all? (13 dishes)

33. Mr. Brown has 4 rows of tulips with 3 tulips in each row. How many tulips does he have in all? (12 tulips)

34. Mrs. Jones paid 80¢ for 4 greeting cards. How much did each card cost? (20¢ each)

35. If Johnny has a bag with 10 gum drops and if he stops at the store and buys 6 more and then he eats 2 on the way home, how many gum drops will Johnny have left? (14 gum drops)

36. Mrs. Davis is having 12 guests for dinner. If she has a loaf of bread with 24 slices, how many slices can Mrs. Davis serve each guest? (2 slices)

37. Farmer Brown has 4 chickens and each chicken lays 2 eggs each day. How many eggs does Farmer Brown collect in one day? (8 eggs)

38. The elevator man went up 7 floors and down 3. What floor was he on if he started on the 1st floor? (5th floor)

39. Bill weighs 85 pounds. When he goes to camp for the summer, he loses 7 pounds at camp. How much does Bill weigh when he goes back to school? (78 pounds)

40. If Sally has 5 dolls and she loses 2 dolls but later finds 1, how many dolls are still missing? (1 doll)

41. A mother hen has 4 black chicks and 5 yellow chicks. How many chicks does she have in all? (9 chicks)

42. There are 3 goldfish in our aquarium. How many more do we need to buy so we will have 10 fish? (7 fish)

43. The mother bird raised two families this spring. In one family there were 3 babies. In the second family there were only 2. How many babies did the mother bird raise? (5 baby birds)

44. We are going to have company for dinner tonight. There will be 5 guests and our family of 6. How many plates will we need? (11 plates)

45. Marcia and John are gathering eggs. They have 7 eggs in their basket. How many more will they need to find to have a dozen eggs? (5 eggs)

46. If Tom was to take 10 books and put them into 2 even piles, how many books would be in each pile? (5 books)

47. Roger weighs 7½ pounds while Bill weighs 2½ pounds less. How much does Bill weigh? (5 pounds)

48. In one of our reading groups we have 10 children. We have only 7 workbooks. How many more do we need so everyone has one? (3 books)

49. Tom worked 12 arithmetic problems. If 8 of them were hard, how many were easy? (4 problems)

50. Mother hen has 7 chicks, and 5 of these chicks are black. The others are yellow. How many chicks are yellow? (2 chicks)

directions and problems for grades 3 and 4

A. This is an exercise in listening as well as in arithmetic problem-solving skills.

B. I will read to you ten questions. Odd-numbered questions such as 1, 3, 5, etc., are easier than the even-numbered questions. You may do only the odd- or even-numbered questions. You may do both if you wish.

C. No grades will be taken on these questions. You will check your own answers.

D. These are nonpaper and nonpencil questions; that is, you listen to the question, think of the answer, and write the answer only on your paper.

E. Number your paper from one to ten. Remember you may choose to do only odd (easier) or even (harder) questions.

F. The questions will be read only once. Listen carefully.

1. Mother made one dozen cookies. If Paul ate 9, how many would be left? (3 cookies)

2. Three boys went to the store to buy bubble gum. Andy bought 8 pieces, Willy bought 15 pieces, and Jane bought 12 pieces. How many pieces did they buy altogether? (35 pieces of gum)

3. Robert had 23 marbles. He won 9 more in a game. How many did he have altogether? (32 marbles)

4. There are 33 students in one third-grade class, and 29 in another. How many students are there in both classes? (62 students)

5. Sally had 15 apples. She ate 2 and gave 6 away. How many did she have left? (7 apples)

6. There are 29 children in Mrs. Brown's third-grade class. If 16 are boys, how many are girls? (13 girls)

7. Bill and Jim went to the rodeo Saturday. They saw 8 white horses and 3 black horses. How many more white horses did they see than black horses? (5 more white horses)

8. Jane brought 2 pints of lemonade to the Thanksgiving party, and Susan brought 1 pint of lemonade. Each pint contains 2 cups. How many cups of lemonade could they serve at the party? (6 cups)

9. Mary went to the grocery store for her mother. She bought 3 boxes of cookies. There were 8 cookies to the box. How many cookies did she buy? (24 cookies)

10. At the end of the sixth inning, the score at the baseball game was 8 for the Redsocks and 5 for the Tigers. In the last inning the Redsocks made 4 runs, and the Tigers made 6 runs. Which team won the game? By how many runs? (Redsocks by 1 run)

11. John went to Mr. Lang's orchard to pick apples. If one bushel of apples weighed 50 pounds, how many would 4 bushels weigh? (200 pounds)

12. Mary has 3 skirts and 4 blouses. How many outfits can she make by using different blouses with each skirt? (12 outfits)

13. A pint is ⅛ of a gallon. How many gallons is 10 pints? (1¼ gallons) 24 pints? (3 gallons) 33 pints? (4⅛ gallons)

14. Mrs. Brown went shopping and bought $12.48 worth of groceries. If she bought 12 items, what was the average cost of each item? ($1.04 each)

15. The distance from Stockton to Lodi is 22½ miles. How many miles is the round trip? (45 miles)

16. If you saved 7¢ of every 20¢ which you earned, how much money would you have saved after you had earned 60¢? (21¢)

17. Ted and John bought a Christmas tree for their parents. Ted wanted to buy a 3 foot, 7 inch tree. John wanted to buy a 4 foot, 6 inch tree. They decided to buy the tree John had picked out. How many inches taller than Ted's tree is John's tree? (11 inches)

18. Mary wanted to buy some ribbon for her new dress. She liked a yellow ribbon which was 21 inches long. She also liked a green ribbon which was 2 feet long. If she bought the longer one, which one did she buy? (green ribbon)

19. There are 12 apples on the table. Three girls want to share the apples equally. How many apples will each girl eat? (4 apples)

20. Three boys went fishing and they caught 21 fish. Bob caught 7 fish. Jerry caught 8 fish. How many fish did Kim catch? (6 fish)

21. Claudia bought 2 yards of material. How many inches of material did Claudia buy? (72 inches)

22. The bus left Stockton at 8:25 A.M. It arrives in Sacramento 1 hour and 25 minutes later. What time will it arrive in Sacramento? (9:50 A.M.)

23. Mary had 4 pies that she wants to cut into pieces so 12 people can have equal shares. How much will each person get? (⅓ of a pie)

24. When Charlie took a trip, it took him ½ hour one way and ⅔ hour on the way back. How many minutes did his trip take? (70 minutes)

25. John has 7 cookies and Stan has 8. They wanted to divide them into 5 groups for their friends. How many cookies did each friend get? (3 cookies)

26. A rug is 4 feet wide and 12 feet long. What is its area? (48 square feet)

27. Harry walked 3¾ miles in the morning and 2¼ miles in the afternoon. How far did he walk altogether? (6 miles)

28. Jim has 59¢. How many stamps at 5¢ each can he buy? (11 stamps with 4¢ left)

29. Six classrooms are to share equally in a shipment of 42 new kickballs received at Terry School. How many kickballs will each classroom receive? (7 kickballs)

30. Karen has 54 photographs taken at Bass Lake last summer. She can put 6 photos on a page in her photo album. How many pages will she fill with the 54 photographs? (9 pages)

31. Jim practiced on his trumpet for 25 minutes on Tuesday and 15 minutes on Wednesday. How many minutes did he practice on both days? (40 minutes)

32. Janice spent 35¢ for lunch each day. How much did it cost her for 5 days? ($1.75)

33. Betty must ride a bus to school. She walks ¾ of a mile to the bus stop. When she gets on the bus, she rides another 2¼ miles to school. How far does Betty live from school? (3 miles)

34. Dennis has 44 boxes all alike in a wagon. The total weight of all the boxes is 132 pounds. How much does each box weigh? (3 pounds)

35. Each person in Mrs. Wilson's class will get 5 pieces of paper. If there are 30 children in the class, how many pieces of paper will Mrs. Wilson need? (150 papers)

36. If a box of apples costs $2.50, how much will 4 boxes cost? ($10)

37. Mr. Smith had 800 peaches to pack in boxes. If he puts 20 peaches in each box, how many boxes will he need? (40 boxes)

38. Sandra had 22 pieces of candy and received 5 more. She then gave 17 pieces away. How many pieces of candy did Sandra have left? (10 candies)

39. How much change will Mary receive from her 25 cents after she buys a pencil for 5¢, paper for 6¢, and candies for 5¢? (9¢)

40. At a Halloween party, 35 children were

grouped in 3s to play a game. How many complete groups of 3 were there? (11 complete groups)

41. Mary has 28 paper dolls. How many will she give away if she gives her sister half of them? (14 paper dolls)
42. Mike placed 16 chairs in each row in the music room. How many chairs did he place in 3 rows? (48 chairs)
43. Ann bought a pair of mittens for 39¢. She gave the clerk 50¢. How much change did she receive? (11¢)
44. The Smiths are traveling 300 miles from the lake to their home. They have gone 248 miles of this journey. How many miles have they still to go? (52 miles)
45. In the number 8,621 what is the value of 2? (2 tens or 20)
46. Two quarts equals how many pints. (4 pints)
47. Which is smaller, 1/8 or 1/16? (1/16)
48. A pie is cut into 8 equal parts and John eats two of them. What fractional part of the pie is left? (¾ or 75%)
49. A baseball team needs 9 players. How many baseball teams can be made up from 27 players? (3 teams)
50. George has 88 pennies, which he wants to exchange for nickels. How many nickels can he get for them? (17 nickels plus 3 pennies or 17.6 nickels)

directions and problems for grades 5 and 6

A. This is an exercise in listening as well as in arithmetic problem-solving skills.
B. I will read to you ten questions. Odd-numbered questions such as 1, 3, 5, etc., are easier than the even-numbered questions. You may do only the odd- or even-numbered questions. You may do both if you wish.
C. No grades will be taken on these questions. You will check your own answers.
D. These are nonpaper and nonpencil questions. That is, you listen to the question, think of the answer, and write only the answer on your paper.
E. Number your paper from one to ten. Remember, you may choose to do only odd (easier) or even (harder) questions.
F. The questions will be read only once. Listen carefully.

1. Jack paid 90¢ for 3 special stamps. How much did each stamp cost? (30¢)
2. Mr. Brown's horse is 15 hands high. A hand is 4 inches. How many feet high is the horse? (5 feet)
3. Tom had 25 marbles, Tim had 50, and Joe had 100 marbles. How many more marbles did Joe have than Tom? (75 marbles)
4. A special super express train in Japan travels 320 miles between Tokyo and Osaka at 160 miles an hour. How many hours does the trip take? (2 hours)
5. If 36 boys are grouped into teams of 9 each, how many teams will there be? (4 teams)
6. A company of soldiers marched 40 miles in five days. The first day they marched 9 miles; the second day, 10 miles; the third day, 6 miles; the fourth day, 8 miles. How many miles did they march on the fifth day? (7 miles)
7. Ned had 24 papers to sell. He sold 9 of them. How many papers has he left to sell? (15 papers)
8. One gallon of gasoline weighs 5.876 pounds. What will 10 gallons of gasoline weigh? (58.76 pounds)
9. Texas has an area of approximately 260,000 square miles and California has an area of approximately 160,000 square miles. How much larger is Texas than California? (100,000 square miles)
10. Jan bought a blouse for $5.25 and a scarf for $1.50. She gave the clerk a ten dollar bill. How much change did she receive? ($3.25)

11. Bob saved $15.98. He spent all but $1.98 of

it for Christmas gifts. How much did he spend on Christmas gifts? ($14)

12. A restaurant owner paid $12.50 for a turkey priced at 50¢ per pound. What was the weight of the turkey? (25 pounds)

13. A small town has 200 parking meters. The average weekly collection from each meter is $2. What would be the total weekly collection? ($400)

14. At the equator the earth's surface moves about 1,000 miles per hour as the earth revolves on its axis. If you lived at the equator, how far would you be carried in a complete day? (24,000 miles)

15. Janet's father earned $120 for a 40-hour work week. What was his hourly rate of pay? ($3.00)

16. The 5,000-mile trip from Seattle to Tokyo required 20 hours of flying time. What was the average speed in miles per hour? (250 mph)

17. Jack's father drives a bus. He has made 150 trips of 100 miles each. How many miles has he driven? (15,000 miles)

18. At 35 miles per hour, how long will it take to drive an automobile a distance of 210 miles? (6 hours)

19. The manager of a school store sold 100 dozen pencils. How many pencils did he sell? (1,200 pencils)

20. A traffic court showed that 615 cars passed a certain point in an hour. At this rate, how many cars would pass in 6 hours? (3,690 cars)

21. About $36,000 is spent each year for paint used on the Golden Gate Bridge. What is the average cost per month? ($3,000)

22. John delivers an average of 200 newspapers a week. At this rate, how many newspapers will he deliver in a year? (10,400 newspapers)

23. A pound of sugar will fill 2¼ cups. How many cups can be filled from a 2-pound package? (4½ cups)

24. A paper company owns 4,000 acres of timber land. In order to increase its landholdings to 400%, how many additional acres must the company buy? (12,000 acres)

25. John and David want to share the cost of a model car kit which costs $3.00. How much will each boy have to pay? ($1.50)

26. A pilot estimating the gasoline needed for a flight allowed a margin of 25% of the total gas needs for safety. If the trip required 200 gallons of gas, how many gallons were put into the tanks? (250 gallons)

27. Kathy wants to go horseback riding, which costs $1.50 for one hour. She can earn 50¢ an hour by babysitting. In how many hours of babysitting can she earn enough for one hour of riding? (3 hours)

28. The enrollment of a small college dropped 5% from a high of 1,000 students. What was the enrollment then? (950 students)

29. Mrs. Garfolo and Mrs. Bartell had 64 pupils between them. Mrs. Garfolo had 40 pupils and Mrs. Bartell had 24. In order for the teachers each to have the same number of pupils in her room, how many should each have? (32 pupils)

30. Bob's father can get a $200 outboard motor at a reduction of $20. What percent is the reduction of the regular price? (10%)

31. Jerry's team scored the following scores in kickball this week: Monday, 3 runs; Tuesday, 4 runs; Wednesday, 0 runs; Thursday, 2 runs; Friday, 1 run. How many runs did Jerry's team score altogether? (10 runs)

32. George's baby brother must be given his bottle every 4 hours. If the baby was last fed at 11:30 A.M., what time will the baby need his next bottle? (3:30 P.M.)

33. David's dog eats a can of dog food a day and the food costs 20¢ per can. How much does it cost to feed the dog per week? ($1.40)

34. Ranger VIII took about 4,000 pictures of the moon during the last 10 minutes of flight. How many pictures a minute did the Ranger camera take? (400 pictures)

35. In arithmetic this week, Candy missed the following number of problems: 3, 4, 5, 1, 2. How many problems did she miss this week? (15 problems)

36. The astronaut, John Glenn, orbited the earth every 1½ hours. How many orbits did he make in 4½ hours? (3 orbits)

37. It takes Jim 5 minutes to walk to school. He also goes home for lunch each day. How much time does Jim spend each day

in walking back and forth to school? (20 minutes)

38. Fire records showed that about 60 out of the last 150 fires were caused by sparks from other fires. What fraction of the fires were caused by such sparks? (2/5)

39. Mary Ann's mother told her to be home at 4:00 P.M. Mary Ann didn't get home until 5:10 P.M. How late was she? (1 hour, 10 minutes)

40. John's class picture costs $1.50 for the large picture. The individual pictures cost 10¢ each if he buys 12 of them. How much should John's mother make the check for if he keeps them all? ($2.70)

41. Kathy's mother told her to bake a double recipe of cookies. This means that Kathy must double all of the measurements. The recipe calls for 1 cup of milk. Will Kathy need a pint or a quart of milk for her cookies? (1 pint)

42. At a market, a sign for apples read: 4 pounds for 20¢. If Mary bought 5 pounds of apples, how much would she have had to pay? (25¢)

43. Jane bought a *Mad* magazine for 60¢ and a *Seventeen* magazine for 80¢. How much did Jane have left out of her $2 allowance? (60¢)

44. If Susan was 9 years old in 1974, how old will she be in 1980? (15 years old)

45. How many hours is a school day that begins at 9:00 A.M. and ends at 3:30 P.M. with an hour out for lunch? (5½ hours)

46. Sam and Jerry were playing marbles. Sam began with 10 marbles and Jerry began with 12. At the end of the game Jerry had lost 3 of his marbles to Sam. Then how many marbles did Sam have? (13 marbles)

47. John wants a driving permit when he is 15½ years. He is now 11½ years. How long must he wait before he applies? (4 years)

48. If in 3 nights Mary slept 10, 6, and 8 hours respectively, what was the average amount of sleep she got per night? (8 hours)

49. In basketball Cincinnati had 30 wins and 12 losses. How many more wins than losses did Cincinnati have? (18 wins)

50. Four boys together bought 2 dozen cookies. They saved half of the cookies, and divided the rest evenly among themselves. How many cookies did each boy get? (3 cookies)

READING WORD PROBLEMS
(grades 2–8)

purposes

To enhance student understanding of word problems

To bring about greater student success in solving word problems

preparation

Select a number of word problems from the textbook or math program, write them on index cards, and arrange them in order from the easiest to the most difficult. (As examples see "Oral Problems for Grades 1–6" in the previous section of this chapter.) Also, make a separate vocabulary list of words, mathematical terms, and symbols which students may not understand.

Measurement Problem 12

Division Problem 5

Money Problem 7

John's father gave him 3 dimes. His mother gave him 2 nickels. How much money did John receive?

(sample problem cards)

Problem Solving Vocabulary

about
account
add
addend
alike
amount
approximate
balance
bankbook

directions

For students to be successful at solving mathematical word problems, they must first be able to read them and then they must understand what is asked. Teachers can help the students improve by having them preview the vocabulary words, mathematical terms, and symbols.

After studying the necessary vocabulary, students should be asked to read the word problems aloud and then *rephrase them in their own words*. Only then can a teacher readily determine whether or not the problems were understood.

Next, the relationships between the mathematical components of a problem need to be analyzed. It is at this point that teachers need to help students consider "reasonable" methods for dealing with the problem facts. At times graphs, tables, estimations, and the like can be helpful, but in the end the student must relate the important facts in a mathematical sentence. The student should then be asked whether the mathematical sentence he has written will likely yield a reasonable answer in terms of the original problem. After a mathematical sentence has been determined, the student needs to compute the answer numerically and consider what that answer means. The final result should then be stated in terms of a total sentence that includes the essential components of the original problem.

A STRATEGY FOR ANALYZING word problems

(grades 3–8)

purposes

To provide a step-by-step method for getting started and working through word problems.

To give the students specific procedures for analyzing and dealing with word problem-solving difficulties

preparation

List the problem-solving steps (see illustration) on the chalkboard, bulletin board, or provide the students with dittoed copies of the Word Problem Analysis worksheet (see Appendix B).

directions

Work through several sample problems with the students using the step-by-step Strategy for Analyzing Word Problems. (See Appendix B for a reproducible Word Problem Analysis worksheet.) Then, tell them that any time they are having difficulty with a word problem they should try this strategy before asking for help. Furthermore, when a student does ask for assistance, work through the entire strategy with her and try to determine where she encounters difficulty. If her difficulty is at a particular step, call this to her attention; and in future problems, she may have to do only that step in a "formal" fashion.

In general, however, do not expect every student to complete every step of the Strategy for Analyzing Word Problems for every problem. Instead, it is intended that the student use it as a means for getting started and for working through "tough spots" in any problem; it is also a diagnostic tool for the teacher.

problem

Nine Girl Scouts are going on a trip to the zoo. One car can hold 6 Girl Scouts. How many will need a ride in another car?

Main Idea (in your own words)   Some Girl Scouts are going in cars to the zoo.
Question   How many Girl Scouts will need to ride in a second car?

Pertinent Facts
   (1) There are 9 Girl Scouts in all.
   (2) One car can hold 6.
   (3) At least 2 cars are needed.

Relationship Sentence (no numbers)   From all of the Girl Scouts take away the number that will ride in the first car, and the rest will have to ride in the second car.
Equation (number sentence) $9 - 6 = \underline{\ ?\ }$
Estimation (without computing)   The answer should be about ____ .
Computation $9 - 6 = \underline{\ 3\ }$
Answer Sentence   At least 3 Girl Scouts will have to ride in the second car. (Note: It is necessary to say "at least 3 Girl Scouts" in this instance because they may choose to have 5 ride in the first car and 4 in the second, etc.)

*See Appendix B, Item 16, for a Word Problem Analysis worksheet that may be reproduced.

oTHER aids For problem solvinG

(grades k-8)

purpose

To provide alternate techniques for interpreting word problems and dealing with everyday problem-solving situations.

preparation

No single strategy can be utilized when attempting to solve the varying types of word problems and applied problem situations. Students must necessarily deal with the appropriate problem-solving aids as they are pertinent to the problem or situation. Thus, selected techniques such as graphing, estimation, equations, tables, and formulas are noted in the following section together with directions for their use.

directions

Any problem situation should be approached in a manner that will help students to understand it. If they "truly" understand what the problem calls for, they should not encounter extreme difficulties when seeking a solution. The Aids for Problem Solving that follow will prove to be helpful in bringing about understanding.

1. estimation

Estimating or making a "good guess" can be helpful in determining the reasonableness of an answer. For example, if your automobile has an 18-gallon gasoline tank and it averages 21.6 miles per gallon, how far will you be able to travel on 1 tank of gasoline? By "rounding" both 18 and 21.6 to 20 we can estimate that we

will be able to travel 400 miles on 1 tank of gasoline. However, even after computing the exact mileage, the wise driver would make a second estimate and not travel more than 350 miles before refueling.

2. graphing

At times graphs can help students to understand the structure of a problem. To illustrate, a kindergarten class might have kept track of the weather for a period of 1 month. During that time it rained on 3 of the days, and was cloudy on 11 other days, and sunny on the rest. The cumulative bar graph portrays this data very vividly. In other instances, line or circle graphs might better illustrate the conditions being considered.

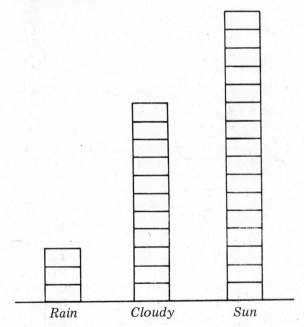

Estimate	*Computation*
	18
20	✕ 21.6
✕ 20	10.8
400	18
	360
	388.8

3. tables

In some instances, especially when limited information is available, setting up a table may help students understand the possible relation-

Number of cars

Jamison	Prouse
8	10
7	9
6	8
5	7
4	6
3	5
2	4
1	3
0	2

ships. For example, if the Prouse family has 2 more cars than the Jamison family, then how many cars could each family own? By arranging a table, we can readily see that if the Jamison family has 2 cars, then the Prouse family has 4, etc. Tables such as this one should, however, be extended only to the extent that the results are reasonable.

4. equations

The information from certain types of problems can readily be displayed via equations. Here is such a problem:

Jim bought 10 candies. Each cost 6¢. How much did all of the candies cost?

10 candies at 6¢ each = _____

or

10 X $.06 = _____

5. formulas

Many problems readily lend themselves to formulation. In one such instance, a home owner might be buying a new carpet for his living room that measures 4 yards by 5 yards. As such, he will need to utilize the formula $A = L \times W$ (area = length $\times$ width) to determine the number of square yards of carpet to purchase.

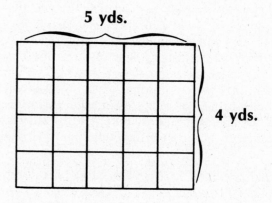

5 yds.

4 yds.

$A = L \times W$
$A = 5 \text{ yds.} \times 4 \text{ yds.}$
$A = 20 \text{ sq. yds.}$

Each of these Aids for Problem Solving can prove to be a valuable tool. However, students will only come to use them proficiently after they have worked with them repeatedly in many varied problem-solving situations.

simulated problems

(grades 1–8)

purposes

To devise "real life" word problems based upon student interests

To help students see applications of mathematics from everyday life

preparation

Through discussion determine specific areas of student interest such as space travel, balanced meals, woodworking, pets, an electrician's job, etc. Then, classify these under major headings (illustrated below are *Everyday Things, Restaurant Menu Math, Catalog Shopping, Science Things, Woodworking and Decorating,* and *Occupations*) and write a series of pertinent problems for each on index cards. Also, be certain that each problem makes use of computation skills pertinent for your students. Finally, devise an answer key that the students may use.

directions

Simulated Problems, utilizing pertinent content skills, should introduce a mathematical content unit of study, be used at least once or twice during the unit, and again at the end of it. In this way the students will come to see problem solving as being related to mathematical content skills rather than as a separate entity. Possible major headings are set forth below together with a sample card for each classification.

Everyday Things	#11

How many cans of moist dog food should you buy? Your dog eats ½ can a day besides table scraps and dry food. You will need enough cans for 1 month.

---

everyday things

A large number of topics might be dealt with under this heading. Some examples might include purchasing snacks, the cost of toys or games, what shoe sizes mean, what electricity costs, how football scores are tallied, how much TV time is advertising, etc.

Restaurant Math	#3

How much will it cost your Dad to buy lunch for you at Your Favorite Restaurant? Get the Restaurant Junior Menu from the wall rack and find the cost for a hamburger, French fries, and milk. If you are really hungry, you can order an ice cream sundae, too.

---

restaurant menu math

Various order combinations from restaurant menus can provide a wealth of computation practice as well as the opportunity to consider those foods in terms of a healthful diet. Such a study might also be expanded to include restaurant management, with the manager of a local restaurant being asked to discuss purchasing, overhead costs, etc.

catalog shopping

A great variety of items can be ordered from Sears, Montgomery Ward, Spiegel, and other catalogs. Thus, one assignment might specifically require the student to order a single item whereas another might be very open ended (i.e., What is the best TV to purchase for your family?). Another interesting approach would be to compare prices in the current catalogs with the 1902 Sears reprint catalog.

Catalog Shopping   #8

What will it cost to order new shoes for each member of your family? Each person will need at least 2 pairs of shoes—one pair for casual wear and another pair for dressing up. Use the catalogs and order forms in the wall rack to complete this task.

---

science things

In this category, topics from space travel to sprouting seeds can be considered. Current items of interest might also range to solar heat, insulation, musical notes, or even sundials. This area of study is limited only by student interests and the creativity of the teacher.

Science   #6

How much heat does a light bulb give off? Get a thermometer and different sizes of light bulbs (25, 40, 60, 75, and 100 watts). Put the 25-watt bulb in a socket and turn it on. Hold the thermometer 1 inch from it for 3 minutes and record the temperature. Do the same for the other bulbs. Also, how hot is a fluorescent lamp?

---

woodworking and decorating

Woodworking situations can readily be adapted for use with operations on fractions. In fact, this is one of the few situations where applied work with common fractions must be completed in an exacting manner.

Decorating is another realm that allows us to relate mathematics in an applied manner to everyday life situations. To begin, students might find out how much paint (or carpet) would be required to redo the classroom and what the cost would be. A more complex task might involve designing and furnishing a complete home.

Woodworking   #16

You have an oak board 74"X6"X1" that you wish to use when making 3 drawer fronts. Each drawer front must be 22¼"X 6"X1". How much oak will remain after cutting the desired lengths on a table saw? (Remember each blade cut causes ⅛" loss.)

occupations

Select a series of occupations that make use of mathematics nearly every day. Ask permission and go to the sites of employment or invite speakers to come to the classroom. The following are just a few of the occupations that use mathematics extensively:

1. Banker—borrowing money, interest on loans, etc.
2. Public accountant—state and federal income tax, property tax, etc.
3. Stockbrokers—investments, bonds, etc.
4. Building contractor—lumber and materials for homes, etc.
5. Insurance agent—home, auto, and life insurance, etc.
6. Department store manager—sales of clothing, sporting goods, determining prices, etc.
7. Decorator—wall coverings, hanging drapes, etc.
8. Trash collector—home, commercial, and disposal area rates, space occupied by trash, etc.
9. Photographer—shutter speeds, lens openings, cost of camera and materials, studio overhead, etc.
10. Real estate agent—measuring lot and home sizes, determining market values, etc.

Occupations   #31

You are to be the new operator of a gas station that sells four types of fuel: premium, regular, unleaded, and diesel. Talk to a service station manager and find out how much of each type fuel he sells each month. How much profit is made per gallon of fuel? What overhead costs are there? Find out as much as you can about operating a gas station. Where do you need mathematics in this occupation?

---

student-devised problems

(grades 3–8)

purposes

To help students to see applications of mathematics related to everyday life

To allow students to illustrate mathematical ideas

To promote a positive attitude toward problem solving

preparation

It is helpful, but not required, to have on hand objects about which word problems may be written. If objects are not available, then pictures or illustrations (sample shown below) may be utilized. Finally, have a supply of index cards available for student use.

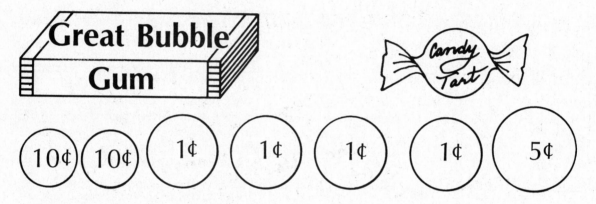

Do I have enough money to treat my 2 friends and myself to 2 candies and 1 stick of gum each? The gum costs 12¢ a package and the candies are 2¢ each. I have 2 dimes, 1 nickel, and 4 pennies. Will I have any extra money?

directions

At the onset place objects before a group of students and work with them to devise several word problems (see sample above) that relate to those objects. After completing several model problems of this type, provide the students with a different set of objects, have each of them devise her own problem, and write it on an index card. Then, have them exchange these problems and see if another student(s) is able to solve it. If difficulties are encountered because the problem was not stated clearly, information was left out, or whatever, have the two students work together (the teacher may also need to assist) to refine the problem until it is in acceptable form.

As students become quite adept at writing their own problems from objects or illustrations, challenge them to go out into the "real world" in search of problems. Such problems will vary according to the age and experiences of the children, but each problem will have explicit meaning for the individual student. A sec-

ond-grade student might be concerned with purchasing a hamster, whereas another in eighth grade might be looking forward to the purchase of a motorcycle. Whatever the problem, however, when students devise, criticize, and refine the problems that they have written themselves, they will begin to see more clearly how many everyday applications and ideas can be illustrated mathematically.

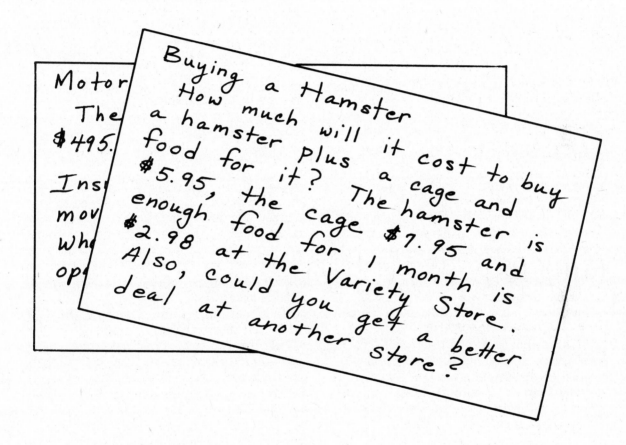

mathematics problem solving in everyday life

(grades 4–8)

purposes

To explore how and why mathematics is done outside school

To encourage estimation and mental computations in applied mathematical situations

preparation

No advance preparation is required. However, a tape recorder may prove to be helpful at times.

directions

Encourage students to find out how adults in various nonschool occupations figure out mathematical problem solutions. For example, they might ask a homemaker, a salesperson, an electrician, a fireman, and anyone else how they would find the answers to questions such as:

1. What is 15% of $8.36?
2. If you owe a bill of $7.32, how much change will you receive from $20.00?
3. If you are making ½ of a recipe which calls for ¼ cup of salad oil, how will you determine the amount of oil to use?
4. If your new car costing $6,489.00 is to be financed at 9.75% for 36 months, how much interest will you pay?

The students should ask the interviewees to verbalize how they think their way through these or other problems. Their responses may be tape-recorded and played back in class if the person agrees. In any event, the teacher and the students should discuss the ways estimation and mental arithmetic are used outside of school. For example, with the problem, "What is 15% of $8.36?" a number of adults may respond something like this: "Ten percent of $8.36 is 84¢ and half of that is 42¢. So, 15% of $8.36 is about $1.26."

While there are some differences in the ways that problem solving is dealt with in and out of school, the two procedures can complement each other. As students continue to explore applied mathematics situations, they should be encouraged and helped to go beyond textbooks and dittoed worksheets. Estimations and mental computations should be encouraged both as adequate processes for certain situations and as a check on "standard" computations (especially those done with hand-held calculators) in others.

problem puzzlers

purposes

To enhance logical thinking skills

To require mental computation and estimations

To encourage a positive attitude toward mathematics

preparation

Collect a series of Problem Puzzlers (samples are shown below). Some of them may be duplicated for distribution to the students.

directions

Problem Puzzlers may be shared verbally or in a duplicated format. In general, however, the shorter problems are presented orally by the teacher and the longer ones distributed to the students for close scrutiny. Thus, this first group of Problem Puzzlers should be presented orally. The answers are found at the end of this section.

1. Take two apples from three apples and what do you have?
2. If an individual went to bed at 8:00 P.M. and set the alarm on a wind-up clock to get up at 9 o'clock in the morning, how many hours sleep would he get?
3. Some months have 30 days, some 31; how many have 28?
4. If your doctor gave you three pills and said to take one every half hour, how long would they last?
5. There are two U.S. coins that total 55¢. One of the coins is not a nickel. What are the two coins?
6. A farmer had 17 sheep. All but 9 died. How many does the farmer have left?
7. Divide 30 by one-half and add 10. What is the answer?
8. How much dirt may be removed from a hole that is 3 feet deep, 2 feet wide, and 2 feet long?
9. There are 12 one-cent stamps in a dozen, but how many two-cent stamps are in a dozen?
10. Do they have a fourth of July in England?
11. A ribbon is 30 inches long. If you cut it with a pair of scissors into one-inch strips, how many snips would it take?
12. How long would it take a train one mile long to pass completely through a mile-long tunnel if the train was going 60 miles per hour?

Some other Problem Puzzlers which are more lengthy or which require pencil and paper computations are cited below. The solutions are noted at the end of this section.

1. *Supreme Court Justices.*

   There are nine Supreme Court Justices. If each shook hands with all of the others, how many handshakes would occur?

2. *Johnson's cat.*

   Johnson's cat went up a tree,
   Which was sixty feet and three;
   Every day she climbed eleven,
   Every night she came down seven,
   Tell me, if she did not drop,
   When her paws would reach the top.

3. *Horse trading.*

There was a sheik in Arabia who had three sons. Upon his death, and the reading of the will, there came about this problem. He had 17 horses. One-half (½) of the horses are willed to his first son. One-third (⅓) are willed to his second son, and 1/9 are willed to his third son. How many horses will each son receive?

4. *Rivers to cross.*

There is an old story about a man who had a goat, a wolf, and a basket of cabbage. Of course, he could not leave the wolf alone with the goat, for the wolf would kill the goat. And he could not leave the goat alone with the cabbage, for the goat would eat the cabbage.

In his travels the man came to a narrow foot bridge which he had to cross. He could take only one thing at a time across the bridge. How did he get the goat, the wolf, and the basket of cabbage across the stream safely?

5. *Jars to fill.*

Mary was sent to the store to buy 2 gallons of vinegar. The storekeeper had a large barrel of vinegar, but he did not have any empty 2-gallon bottles. Looking around, he found an 8-gallon jar and a 5-gallon jar. With these 2 jars he was able to measure out exactly 2 gallons of vinegar for Mary. How?

6. *A vanishing dollar.*

A farmer was driving his geese to market. He had 30 geese, and he was going to sell them at 3 for $1.
"That is 33⅓¢ apiece," he figured, "and 30 times 33⅓¢ is $10."

On his way to market, he passed the farm of a friend who also raised geese. The friend asked him to take his 30 geese along and sell them, too; but, since they were large

and fat, he wanted them sold at 2 for $1.
"That is 50¢ apiece," the farmer said to his friend, "so your geese will bring 30 times 50¢, or $15."
After leaving his friend, the farmer figured, "It would be a lot simpler to sell all 60 geese at a single price. Now 3 for $1 and 2 for $1 are the same as 5 for $2."

So the farmer decided to sell all the geese at the rate of 5 for $2. And that's exactly what he did.

On his way home he gave his neighbor the $15 due him. Then he thought, "When I get home, I'll give my wife the $10 that I got for our geese."

But when he looked in his pocket, he was surprised to find that he had only $9 instead of $10.

He looked all over for the missing dollar, but he never did find it. What became of it?

Answers to Problem Puzzlers presented orally:

(1) 2 apples
(2) 1 hour
(3) all
(4) 1 hour
(5) 50¢ piece + nickel
(6) 9 sheep
(7) 70
(8) None—the hole has no dirt itself.
(9) 12
(10) yes
(11) 29 snips. The last two inches are divided by one snip.
(12) Two minutes. From the time the front of the train enters the tunnel to the time the back of the train leaves the tunnel, the train must travel two miles. At 60 mph, the train is going a mile a minute.

Answers to Problem Puzzlers which are more lengthy or which require pencil and paper computations:

(1) Thirty-six handshakes.
(2) Each day the cat went up 11 feet and came

(grades 5–8)

down 7. So she moved 4 feet a day. In 13 days the cat climbed 4 × 13, or 52 feet; then on the 14th day her paws reached the top, since 52 + 11 = 63.

(3) Possible solutions:

1/2 × 17/1 = 8 1/2 = 9 horses for 1st son
1/3 × 17/1 = 5 2/3 = 6 horses for 2nd son
1/9 × 17/1 = 1 8/9 = 2 horses for 3rd son
17 horses

(4) Takes goat across; returns. Takes wolf across; brings back goat. Takes cabbage across; returns. Takes goat across.

(5) (Call 8-gal. jar A and 5-gal. jar B).
Fill B; empty B into A. Fill B. Fill A from B. There are 2 gallons left in B.

(6) $10 + $15 = $25
5 for $2 = 40¢ each
60 × 40¢ = $24

CHAPTER X

USING Hand-Held calculators

⊙⊙⊙⊙⊙⊙⊙⊙⊙⊙⊙⊙⊙⊙⊙⊙⊙⊙

Now that hand-held calculators have become reasonably priced, they are appearing in the hands of many elementary school students. As such, the question of whether they should be allowed in classrooms has really changed to "how can we use them most wisely?" Calculators should *not* be offered in place of mathematical understanding; rather, they should be used as teaching aids that can motivate students to learn basic concepts. Students who are to be using calculators need to understand the basic mathematical processes—addition, subtraction, multiplication, and division—before they are allowed to use them extensively. That is to say, students should be allowed to use calculators in school classrooms only after they understand what the calculators are doing for them.

The first section of this chapter, Selecting Hand-Held Calculators for Classroom Use, may serve as a guide when purchasing calculators. The next three portions—Classroom Uses for Hand-Held Calculators, Practicing Basics with Hand-Held Calculators and Developing Estimation Skills for Use with Hand-Held Calculators—give specific methods for classroom utilization of calculators. Then, the final three sections—Problem Solving with Calculators, Hand-Held Calculators in the Grocery Store, and Write Your Own Calculator Problems—cite examples where calculators might be used to help solve "real life" problems.

In addition to those described here, certain activities from other portions of this book might also be accomplished with the

⊙⊙⊙⊙⊙⊙⊙⊙⊙⊙⊙⊙⊙⊙⊙⊙⊙⊙⊙⊙⊙⊙⊙⊙⊙⊙⊙⊙⊙

aid of hand-held calculators. Included might be Add 'Em Up and Palindromic Addition in Chapter III, Stay Out of the Hole and One Thousand and One from Chapter IV, Tangle Tables in Chapter V, Averaging Activities and Division Squares from Chapter VI, Calculating and Comparing in Chapter VII, Capture a Numeral and Operation 500 from Chapter VIII, and Student-Devised Problems from Chapter IX.

selecting hand-held calculators for classroom use

(grades k–8)

purposes

To determine which calculator features are important for your students

To indicate selected procedures that may be completed with hand-held calculators

preparation

In order to determine which hand-held calculator best fits the needs of your classroom, you will want to try out several different makes and models. This can be done by having your school sales representative request the loan of demonstration calculators or by simply stopping at the calculator/office machines counters of several discount or variety stores.

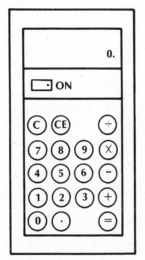

A basic hand-held calculator

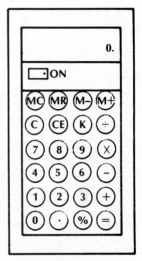

A calculator with extra features

directions

When selecting a hand-held calculator for classroom use, note which features are essential and which would be nice to have. Each manufacturer utilizes a keyboard that is arranged in a slightly different manner; but the essential keys are those shown in the "basic calculator" illustration. Other essential features include:

1. *Algebraic logic.* This means, for example, that the answer to 5 + 3 = is obtained by pressing the keys in just that way.
2. *Four functions.* The calculator should +, –, ×, and ÷ with separate keys.
3. *No key should have a dual purpose.* This includes the C key for clearing the calculator and the CE key which clears only the last entry.
4. *Eight-digit readout.* This is important when working with money in order that, for example, the answer display may extend into the hundred thousands such as $396,427.86.

5. *Easy to read display.* The answer display numerals should be large enough to read easily and the display surface should be such that it does not glare when viewed at a slight angle.
6. *Floating decimal.* Try a problem such as 5 ÷ 3 and, if the answer is displayed as 1.6666666, the calculator has this feature; but if it is shown as 1.66, it does not.
7. *Rechargeable unit or AC adapter.* Calculators that can be recharged overnight or plugged in during use are much better for classroom use than those that use batteries that must be replaced constantly.

Certain additional features are sometimes very helpful. The illustration for "a calculator with extra features" displays the supplementary keys that are found on certain hand-held calculators. Thus, the extra features might include:

1. *Constant.* This is usually indicated by the

Letter K on one of the keys (also a few calculators have an automatic constant). The K function allows the operator to key a number into the calculator one time and then proceed to do repeated operations on that number. For example, a student might multiply 127 by a series of different numbers without having to punch the 1, 2, 7, and multiply keys each time.

2. *Memory.* Some hand-held calculators utilize a memory feature which allows the operator to store a number for later use, add to or subtract from it, and to recall it simply by pressing the proper keys. Thus, to store a number that is shown on the display simply press M+ (memory plus), to recall it later on press MR (memory recall), to subtract a new display number from it press M– (Memory minus), to add to it use M+ again, and the cumulative total is recalled at any time via MR. Finally, when the memory number is no longer needed press MC (memory clear).

3. *Floating negative sign.* This is nice to have but not essential. If the calculator displays a negative four as –4 rather than –   4, it has the floating decimal feature. With it, students are less likely to omit needed negative signs.

4. *Keys that click.* Spring-loaded keys that click may help a student to know whether or not he has pressed the key firmly enough so that the number has registered.

5. *Percent Key.* Many calculators have a % key which simply eliminates having to punch additional keys. For example, 6% of $12 would require the student to press the 1, 2, ✕, 6, and % keys to yield .72 instead of the 1, 2, ✕, •, 0, and 6 keys for the same result.

Also, decide how many calculators could best be used in your classroom. A calculator for each student is not essential; in fact, just one calculator can be very helpful in a mathematics center, to use for checking answers, as a substitute for flash cards or other aids. Just how many calculators you should purchase is probably best determined by available funds and how much time you want each student to make use of one. However, one hand-held calculator for every four or five students is probably sufficient for most classrooms.

Finally, whether you purchase one or more calculators for use in your classroom, be certain to try out the calculators from various manufacturers and utilize the guidelines suggested above to determine which features would help (or hinder) your particular students. Also, be certain to choose a reliable company that will provide service if the calculator should need it.

cLASSROOM USES
foR HANd—HELd cALcuLATORS

(grades k–8)

purposes

To help students utilize hand-held calculators as alternate computational aids

To describe varied methods for utilizing hand-held calculators in classrooms

preparation and directions

Now that hand-held calculators have become so reasonably priced—less than $20 for one with a memory function, and less than $10 for a good basic calculator—they are appearing in the hands of a great many students. The question of whether we should use them has really changed to "How can we make the best use of them?"

The calculator is not a magic device, but rather one that rapidly completes your basic computations if you know which numbers to use and how to key them in. Thus, the student using a calculator must still understand the processes and know the meanings for the basic facts—addition, subtraction, multiplication, and division. That is to say that a student should use a calculator only after she understands what the calculator is doing for her.

This section will briefly describe possible classroom uses for hand-held calculators. Some of these methods will also receive additonal emphasis in later sections of the chapter. Thus, selected classroom uses for calculators might include:

1. *Counting and numeral identification.*

    Children soon learn that they can count almost effortlessly by any number. For example, if they enter 1 + 1 which equals 2 and continue to press the = button they will proceed as 1, 2, 3, 4, 5, 6, 7, 8, 9, 10, 11 ... The same is true when counting by 4 when 4 + 4 = 8 and the sequence becomes

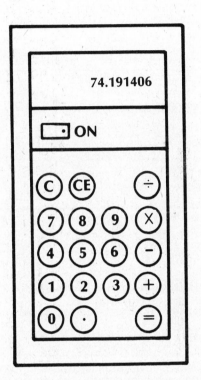

4, 8, 12, 16, 20, etc., when the = button is again pressed repeatedly.

Numeral identification can also be practiced with the teacher (or another student) naming a numeral and the student pressing the keys in the proper order to name that number. For example, if the teacher says thirty-one the student's calculator display would need to appear as 31, not 13 or some other numeral arrangement, in order to be correct. Also, a series of such numerals could be added together, and if upon pressing the = sign the student's total matches the teacher's (such as 31 + 43 + 17 + 29 = 120), then she has identified the numerals correctly.

2. *Basic fact practice.*

A calculator may be used instead of flash cards when practicing basic addition, subtraction, multiplication, or division facts. When doing so have one child call out fact such as 7 + 8 and punch it into the calculator. As soon as the other student has answered, she should press the = button to find out whether the student answered correctly.

By using a calculator with a built-in constant function, a higher level of basic drill can take place. Suppose you want to practice multiplying by 8. To do so, press in the 8 and X buttons (and K on some calculators) and hand it to the student, telling him to find out what number you multiplied by. By trial and error she might record:

$$X\ 3 = 24$$
$$X\ 5 = 40$$
$$X\ 7 = 56$$
$$X\ 2 = 16$$

By this time she has likely determined that she is multiplying by 8.

A more detailed description as to how basic facts might be practiced with a calculator is set forth in a later section of this chapter titled Practicing Basics with Hand-Held Calculators.

3. *Understanding computation.*

Hand-held calculators can help to develop an understanding of basic algorithms through the use of repeated operations. Try the following examples to see how this can be done:
   (a) Add 67 nine times. How does this compare with 9 X 67?
   (b) Complete ? X 96 = 3,648 without dividing (hint: how many 96s added together make 3,648)
   (c) Prove your division answer for 63 ÷ 7 by also finding out how many 7s can be subtracted from 63.
   (d) Find a number that you can divide 149 by that will yield a remainder of 5. Can

you find a second divisor that will give the same remainder?

This process will also be dealt with in more detail later in this chapter in the section titles Practicing Basics with Hand-Held Calculators.

4. *Estimating.*

Teachers have often asked students to give an estimate of the possible answer or to determine whether an answer that has already been computed is sensible. However, with the advent of hand-held calculators these skills have become more important than ever before. A student faced with the problem 47 X 612 must first round these factors to 50 X 600, as well as knowing the answer to 5 X 6, before she can estimate the answer to be near 30,000. Without such skills the student will operate "blindly" and simply accept any answer that the calculator displays. In order that students may become more adept at estimating and determining the reasonableness of answers selected, activities to enhance these skills are set forth in a later section of this chapter titled Developing Estimation Skills for Use with Hand-Held Calculators.

5. *Verifying solutions.*

A hand-held calculator may be used as a portable answer key by either the students or the teacher when checking pencil and paper computations. However, this is a very limited use, and it does in some cases have disadvantages. Consider, for example, a student who has painstakingly worked a multiplication problem such as 3,597 X 2,794 and arrived at an incorrect solution because her columns were not aligned. By contrast, she worked the same problem on the calculator in a few seconds and thus decided that the pencil and paper method of computation was totally unreal.

On a broader scale calculators might be used to verify mental arithmetic solutions. Thus, for an oral problem such as 8, +3, −9, X 2, ÷ 2, +36, the students would need to mentally arrive at the same answer as displayed on the calculator.

Another verification process might involve "debugging" problems. For example, find the missing portions in these problems:

```
  _4          1_6
 +5_         +23_
 ――――        ――――
  98          _04
```

```
   85
 X 6_
 ――――                      864375
  595                 .08 |‾69.15
 51_0
 ――――
 5__5
```

6. *Problem solving.*

Use the calculator to assist with the solutions for word problems and everyday problems from the "real world." By doing so students will not be deterred by computation processes, but they must still understand when certain operations need to take place. A typical textbook word problem where a calculator might prove to be helpful is:

> I bought 15 pieces of cloth, each 12 yards long, at $1.82 per yard. What was the total cost?
>
> Solution: 15 X 12 X $1.82 = $327.60

"Real world" problems are also solved with much greater ease through using hand-held calculators. During a period of water shortage, for example, let us consider how much water is lost from a faucet that drips day after day:

> How many gallons of water will be lost in 1 year if the faucet is not fixed? A container set under it retained 3¼ cups of water after a 24-hour period.

(hint: 1 gallon = 16 cups)

Solution: $\dfrac{3\frac{1}{4} \text{ cups} \times 365\frac{1}{4}}{16 \text{ cups per gallon}}$

or

(3.25 X 365.25) ÷ 16 = 74.19
gallons of water lost per year

Further situations dealing with ways to use calculators in relation to word problems and real world problems are discussed in three later sections of this chapter. Those three sections are titled Problem Solving with Calculators, Hand-Held Calculators in the Grocery Store, and Write Your Own Calculator Problems.

7. *Calculator games.*

Such games may be played in several different formats including races, estimating answers, and logical thinking processes. A race-type game might involve one student using a calculator and several who are not. Those without calculators try to write the answer to a problem such as 7 X 8 or 23 X 11 before the other student can show the answer on the calculator.

An estimation game would involve a similar process except that the students need not race, large problems are utilized, and the students without calculators are allowed to estimate solutions within 1,000 (or any reasonable limit) of the answer. Thus, for a problem such as 395 X 812, those estimating would get credit for estimates within 1,000 of the exact answer— 320,740.

Activities such as Palindromic Sums (found in Chapter III, "Addition") can also be modified for use with a hand-held calculator. Students may compete to see who can find the Palindromic or reversible sum which took the greatest number of steps to attain.

For example, if one student starts with 273 and another with 380, the steps are shown below:

$$
\begin{array}{r}
273 \\
+372 \\
\hline
645 \\
+546 \\
\hline
1{,}191 \\
+1{,}911 \\
\hline
3{,}102 \\
+2{,}013 \\
\hline
5{,}115
\end{array}
\qquad\qquad
\begin{array}{r}
380 \\
+083 \\
\hline
463 \\
+364 \\
\hline
827 \\
+728 \\
\hline
1{,}555 \\
+5{,}551 \\
\hline
7{,}106 \\
+6{,}017 \\
\hline
13{,}123 \\
+32{,}131 \\
\hline
45{,}254
\end{array}
$$

Palindromic Sum in 4 steps

Palindromic Sum in 6 steps

Another game might involve two students who must utilize logical guessing. To play, pick two numbers—one over 1,000 and the other less than 100; let's say 3,645 and 27. The players must then guess what number multipled by 27 will yield 3,645. Player 1 might try $120 \times 27 = 3{,}240$. Her answer is 405 too small; therefore, she must record 405 on her score sheet. Player 2 then tries $140 \times 27 = 3{,}780$. Since she is 135 over, she must record this on her sheet. Play returns to Player 1 who tries $135 \times 27 = 3{,}645$. Since she determined the correct answer, she is allowed a bonus of 100 which she may subtract from her total. Thus, Player 1 has $405 - 100 = 305$ as compared with Player 2 who has 135. Therefore, Player 2, because her score is the lowest, is the winner.

pRacticing basics with hand-held calculators

(grades 1–8)

purposes

To reinforce basic concepts and skills relating to numbers, counting, place value, addition, subtraction, multiplication, division, fractions, and decimals

To increase student interest in learning basic mathematical concepts and skills

preparation

From one to ten hand-held calculators need to be readily available to the students in your classroom. In specific situations, where noted, manipulative materials and pencils and paper will also be needed to augment the calculators.

directions

As a teacher there are many calculator techniques you may utilize to help students understand basic concepts and to encourage them to practice the related skills. Some pertinent suggestions, together with brief comments and examples relating to them, are noted here.

1. *Numbers and Counting.*

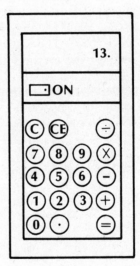

During early exposure to hand-held calculators, relate the children's experiences to manipulative and pictorial materials. For example, lay thirteen plastic straws on a student's desk and have him count them both by manipulation and by 1-to-1 correspondence on the calculator. Thus, through repeated adding the calculator will display an answer of 13. Ask him then to use the straws and a rubber band to show what the 1 and the 3 in the 13 really mean.

He should be able to show 3 single straws and one bundle of 10 straws as illustrated above. (Further practice with such skills may be accomplished by using calculators along with the Straw Count and Egg Carton Math activities described in Chapter I.) As the student becomes more proficient, he may use the calculator to help him count by

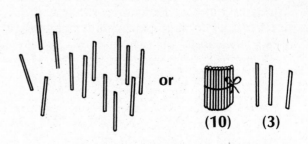

5s, 10s, 3s, or whatever. When counting by 5s he may proceed verbally 5, 10, 15, 20 and then become "stuck." At this point he may use the calculator to enter $5 + 5 = 10$ and

then repeatedly press the $=$ button to yield $= 15, = 20, = 25$, etc. He could also be asked to draw a picture of 25, and it might appear as:

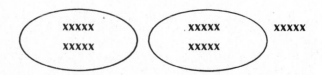

2. *Place Value.*

The example with 13 in the Numbers and Counting section above illustrates a beginning method for dealing with place value. However, a verbally oriented calculator activity may cause students to gain further understanding. To begin, two or more students will need calculators. Then the teacher calls out a rule and several numerals—perhaps 8, 6, 2, and 7—with the stipulation that they show a numeral with place value nearest 7,000. The students are allowed a set amount of time to enter the numerals into the calculator. One student might display 7,268 and another 6,872. If the student with 6,872 can correctly tell the number of hundreds, tens, thousands, and ones as well as how near 7,000 his numeral is, he becomes the winner.

In another setting a student might be challenged to find all of the place value ar-

rangements for a certain set of numerals such as 2, 3, and 7. He will need to use pencil and paper, as well as a calculator, in

$$
\begin{array}{r}
237 \\
273 \\
372 \\
327 \\
732 \\
+\ 723 \\
\hline
2,664
\end{array}
$$

order to keep track as he records all possibilities. As soon as he thinks he has found them all, he adds on the calculator to determine their sum. If his answer matches the teacher's, and he can correctly name each numeral, his answer wins. (Other place value activities that can be enhanced by using a calculator are Straw Trading, Place Value Trip, and Find A Million from Chapter II.)

3. *Addition and Subtraction.*

Basic addition and subtraction facts can be practiced by two students working with a calculator. To do so, one should call out a fact such as $11 - 6$ and enter it into the calculator. As soon as the other student has given an answer, the $=$ button is pressed; and, immediately, it is known whether or not the response was correct. Any problems answered incorrectly should be recorded on paper and practiced again later.

If the calculator has a constant feature (either built-in or with a K key), the teacher may enter a constant situation such as $+8$ (or -7) and hand the calculator back to the student, telling him to find the number that is being added (or subtracted) in each instance. The student must repeatedly enter numbers and an equal sign until the missing numeral is determined, such as:

Number Entered		Number Displayed	
5	=	13	(___ + 5 = 13)
12	=	20	(___ + 12 = 20)
7	=	15	(___ + 7 = 15)

Still another technique is to ask students to find missing numerals in addition and subtraction problems. When completing problems such as those below, the calculator serves to help with calculations and to verify solutions that have been determined through logical thinking.

$$
\begin{array}{r} 38 \\ + \underline{} \\ \hline 61 \end{array}
\qquad
\begin{array}{r} 1\ 5 \\ 68 \\ +137 \\ \hline 26 \end{array}
\qquad
\begin{array}{r} 372 \\ - \underline{} \\ \hline 81 \end{array}
\qquad
\begin{array}{r} \$5.00 \\ -\ 3. \\ \hline \$1.70 \end{array}
$$

(Other addition activities, which might be modified for calculator use, are Spill A Sum, Add 'Em Up, and Palindromic Addition from Chapter III. Selected subtraction activities might include Bean Toss Subtraction, Stay Out of the Hole, and One Thousand and One from Chapter IV.)

4. *Multiplication and Division.*

Basic multiplication and division facts can be practiced on the calculator in flash card fashion. That is, one student should enter a basic fact into the calculator, such as 6 X 9 (or 72 ÷ 8), and as soon as his partner has given an answer, the = sign is pressed to flash the correct response on the display. Also, the answer can be verified through repeated addition (or subtraction for 72 ÷ 8) such as 9+9+9+9+9+9 = 54.

Calculators can also be helpful when trying to determine missing factors. For example, 8 X ___ = 64 may be found by trial and error multiplication or by a single division. Missing components, such as those below, can also be determined by logical thinking and help from a calculator:

$$
\begin{array}{r} 3\_ \\ \times\ \_4 \\ \hline \_40 \\ 700 \\ \hline 840 \end{array}
\qquad
\begin{array}{r} \_6 \\ \_6\,\overline{\smash{)}\,3\_8} \\ \underline{-36} \\ 2 \end{array}
\qquad
\begin{array}{r} 7545 \\ .06\,\overline{\smash{)}\,45.27} \end{array}
$$

(Where does the answer decimal belong?)

By utilizing a calculator with a constant (K) feature, the teacher may enter a multiplication (or division) rule and ask the student to determine it. For example, if the teacher had pressed the 4, X, and K buttons the students' calculations might appear as:

Number Entered		Number Displayed	
5	=	20	(___ X 5 = 20)
8	=	32	(___ X 8 = 32)
2	=	8	(___ X 2 = 8)

As such, the student should soon be able to determine that the rule was *4 × number =* *answer*. A similar process for division using the rule *divide by 5* might appear as:

Number Entered		Number Displayed	
10	=	2	(10 ÷ ____ = 2)
20	=	4	(20 ÷ ____ = 4)
28	=	5.6	(28 ÷ ____ = 5.6)
50	=	10	(50 ÷ ____ = 10)
5	=	1	(5 ÷ ____ = 1)

(Other selected activities where calculators may be utilized for multiplication and division are Tangle Tables and Hookey in Chapter V plus Divide to Get Home, Averaging Activities, and Division Squares in Chapter VI.)

5. *Fractions and Decimals.*

For years common fractions have been used widely; but, with the coming of the metric system and the advent of inexpensive hand-held calculators, decimal fractions will replace them in many instances. Thus, students need to work with decimal fractions in several formats. One way to begin is to use the calculator to help devise a chart such as the one below:

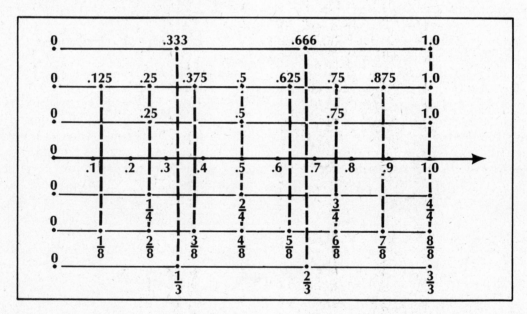

Notice that the common fractions below the decimal number line are related to the decimal fractions above it and are connected by the dashed lines. (Example: Note that ⅛ = 8 ÷ 1 = .125.) As the students and the teacher use calculators to devise such a chart, they will no doubt become more proficient with both common and decimal fractions. It is likely that they will also come to see how much easier it would be to relate all fractions as decimal tenths, hundredths, and thousandths.

Another problem that students have sometimes encountered when working with common fractions is determining which of two fractions is larger. As an example, 1/6 may seem smaller than 1/9 because 9 is a greater numeral; but, a quick check with the calculator shows $1/6 = 6 \div 1 = .166 \ldots$, which is greater than $1/9 = 9 \div 1 = .111 \ldots$ Fractions such as ⅔ and ⅝ are even more difficult to envision, but again the calculator can quickly show ⅔ $= .666 \ldots$, which is greater than ⅝ $= .625$.

One final consideration, which will be dealt with here, is where to put the decimal point when multiplying and dividing numerals such as 3.54, .06, and .95. Problems of this type are noted below. Use your calculator to quickly determine whether the decimal points are in the correct locations.

(A)
$$5.95 \\ \underline{\times .06} \\ .357$$

(B)
$$16.20 \\ \underline{\times .25} \\ .405$$

(C)
$$6312.85 \\ \underline{\times .1075} \\ 678.63$$

(D) $2.5 \overline{\smash{)}15.65}$ with quotient $.626$

(E) $4.8 \overline{\smash{)}0.56}$ with quotient 1.1666666

(F) $89.37 \overline{\smash{)}12{,}657.00}$ with quotient 14162

(Other fraction and decimal activities with which hand-held calculators may be utilized are Calculating and Comparing, Match a Fraction, and Fraction and Decimal Magic Squares from Chapter VII.)

developing estimation skills for use with hand-held calculators

(grades 3–8)

purposes

To develop skills for rounding numbers and estimating

To extend students' estimating skills to word problems and "real life" problem-solving situations

preparation

Pencil and paper as well as hand-held calculators should be available for student use.

directions

Estimation is a crucial skill which can be utilized in nearly every facet of mathematics both in and out of school. In many situations a good estimate will serve as well as a precise answer. To estimate accurately, students must first learn how to round numbers. While pencil and paper or hand-held calculators may be of assistance, most estimating must be completed mentally. To begin, consider rounding in the following situations:

1. *Rounding to the nearest 10.*

   As you round each number, enter it into the calculator and press the + button. When finished, use the calculator again to tally the true answer. If your estimate was within 10, you did a good job.

   (a) $7 + 21 + 8 + 14 + 19 = $ ____ (est. = 70, ans. = 69)

   (b) $97 + 83 + 68 + 70 + 54 = $ ____ (est. = 380, ans. = 379)

   (c) $421 + 387 + 512 + 26 + 391 = $ ____ (est. = 1,740, ans. = 1,737)

2. *Rounding to the nearest 100.*

   As you round each of these numbers to the nearest 100, enter them into the calculator and press the + button. When finished, your estimated answer should be within 100 of the true answer.

   (a) $437 + 581 + 612 + 457 + 502 = $ ____ (est. = 2,600, ans. = 2,589)

   (b) $1,166 + 5,031 + 8,965 + 2,317 + 1,100 = $ ____ (est. = 18,600, ans. = 18,579)

   (c) $30,006 + 25,972 + 16,384 + 14,212 + 42,959 = $ ____ (est. = 129,600, ans. = 129,533)

160

3. *Rounding answers.*

In many instances a calculator will give more precise decimal answers than are needed. Thus, round each of the answers to the problems given to two decimal places:

(a)
$$\begin{array}{r} 35.16 \\ \times\ \ 7.54 \\ \hline 265.1064 \end{array}$$

(b)
$$3\overline{\smash{\big)}\,2000} = 666.66667$$

(c)
$$37.12\overline{\smash{\big)}\,465.21} = 12.532597$$

(265.11)

(66.67)

(12.53)

the calculator may be of assistance when working on such problems. An example of a primary grade problem and another for

When students are able to round numbers and answer quite accurately, they should be guided into using these same skills in conjunction with word problems. Again, intermediate grade students, together with explanatory notes, are shown below:

(a) *World problem for primary students*

How many marbles do the children have in all? Jim has 36 marbles, Sara has 28, Pat has 14, and Danny has 9.

(Note: Many first-grade children can solve problems such as this with help from a calculator. The estimate would be 40 + 30 + 10 + 10 = about 90 marbles in all. The calculated answer tells us that the children actually had 87 marbles in all.)

(b) *Word problem for intermediate students.*

How much will it cost to repair John's bicycle? It needs a new seat costing $6.85, a fender at $5.35, and a pedal at $4.15. Also, there is a sales tax of 6% on all items.

(Note: The estimate would be $7 + $5 + $4 = $16. Thus, we would expect the repairs to cost about $16. By calculating, we find $6.85 + $5.35 + $4.15 = $16.35. Also, the sales tax is $16.35 X .06 = $.981. Therefore, the cost of repairing the bicycle will be $16.35 + .98 = $17.33.)

Finally, the calculator can be most valuable when applying estimating skills to "real world" problem-solving situations. Only the teacher's creativity and the students' interests will limit the problems and proposed solutions that may be dealt with in everyday life. To cite a possible example:

Bread loaves

How many loaves of bread do the people in your town eat in one year? You will need to find estimates for the number of slices that are in an average loaf of bread, how many slices most people eat per day, and approximately how many people live in your town. Then, use a calculator to compute your estimated answer.

Additional problems, in both word problem and "real life" settings, are set forth in the Problem Solving with Calculators section of this chapter.

problem solving with calculators

(grades 3–8)

purposes

To allow students to work with and solve both word problems and "real world" problems that would ordinarily require higher-level computation skills than they might possess

To help students see applications of mathematics from everyday life

preparation

Note specific areas of student interest and then locate, modify, and devise problems for them to try. The students must understand the computational processes that the problems will require them to complete, but by using a calculator they will be able to deal with computation of a large magnitude (if a student understands 4 × 6, she can use the calculator to accomplish 400 × 600, etc.).

directions

In a process such as this, the teacher must assign problems that are at the proper level of difficulty for individual students. The initial problems should probably be of the word or story problem type with a single solution. As the students become more adept, however, the problems can be much more open-ended. Of the four problems noted below, *Buying School Supplies* and *Purchasing a Bicycle* are variations on the former description whereas *Money from Baby Sitting* and *Building a House* are of the latter.

Calculator Work

$$
\begin{array}{r}
\$ \quad .20\ + \\
.79\ + \\
.59\ + \\
.99\ + \\
.39\ = \\
\hline
\$\ \ 2.96
\end{array}
$$

$$
\begin{array}{r}
\$\ \ 9.87\ \times \\
12\ = \\
\hline
\$118.44
\end{array} \quad \text{(cost for 12 payments)}
$$

$$
\begin{array}{r}
\$118.44\ - \\
109.54\ = \\
\hline
\$\ \ 8.90
\end{array}
$$

You will save $8.90 by paying the cash price.

Problem

1. *Buying school supplies.*

   Jennifer and her mother went to the variety store to buy school supplies. She bought 4 pencils for 20¢, a large tablet for 79¢, a ruler for 59¢, a box of crayons for 99¢, and a large eraser for 39¢. How much did these school supplies cost?

2. *Purchasing a bicycle.*

   A new ten-speed bicycle will cost $109.54 including tax. If you don't have enough money to pay for it now, you can make 12 monthly payments of $9.87. How much do save if you pay cash?

$$\begin{array}{r} \$ \ .75 \times \\ \underline{4 =} \\ \$ \ 3.00 \end{array}$$ (Friday night)

- - - -

$$\begin{array}{r} \$ \ .90 \times \\ \underline{4 =} \\ \$ \ 3.60 \end{array}$$ (Saturday night)

- - - -

$$\begin{array}{r} \$ \ 3.00 + \\ \underline{3.60 =} \\ \$ \ 6.60 \end{array}$$ (each weekend)

- - - -

$$\begin{array}{r} \$85.47 \div \\ \underline{6.60 =} \\ \$12.95 \end{array}$$ (weeks)

- - - -

3. *Money from baby-sitting.*

Pat works as a baby-sitter for 4 hours each Friday and Saturday night. She gets 75¢ per hour on Friday and 90¢ per hour on Saturday. She wants to buy a bicycle which costs $85.47, including tax. How many weeks will she have to work before she can buy the bicycle?

It will take Pat at least 13 weeks to earn enough money for the bicycle.

4. *Building a house.*

What will it cost to build a new house? You will need to draw your house plan to scale and then figure what it will cost to construct it. Here are some of the things you will need to consider:

(a) Drawing plans—the teacher will need to orient the students to (rough) scale drawings, using drawing instruments, roof pitch, window sizes, etc.
(b) Materials and labor—you may wish to talk with a contractor about cost per square foot, etc.
(c) Measurements—such as board feet, grades of wood, cubic yards of concrete, etc.
(d) Electrical plans
(e) Plumbing and heating plans
(f) Doors and windows
(g) Wall and ceiling covering
(h) Floor covering
(i) Tile, carpet, and drapes
(j) Cabinets
(k) Paint
(l) Total cost—add up all expenses and divide by the number of square feet in your house to find your cost per square foot.

hand-held calculators in the grocery store

(grades 5–8)

purposes

To utilize calculators when solving mathematical problems from the "real world"

To provide "hands-on" experience with the mathematics of grocery shopping

---

SUCCESSFUL BUDGETS BEGIN HERE ◄

GRAPEFRUIT JUICE	46-Oz. Can 49¢
PEACHES	2½ Can, Sliced or Halves 39¢
CAT FOOD	6-Oz 4 for $1
PICKLES	22-Oz. Jar 89¢
GRANOLA Sun Country	1-lb. Box 79¢

PEPSI COLA

16-Oz. 8-Pack Ctn.

$1.09 plus tax

BANANAS

4 LBS $1

ASPARAGUS	47¢ lb.
CABBAGE	19¢ lb.
LETTUCE	Large Head 29c
ARTICHOKES	Select 4 for $1
CUCUMBERS	4 for $1

MUSHROOMS

79¢ lb.

BONELESS STEW MEAT .... $1.29 lb.

LONDON BROIL STEAK .... $1.69 lb.

Real McCoy, 8-Oz. Pkg.
BEEF LINK SAUSAGE .... 49¢ ea

12-Oz. Pkg.
Turkey Bologna or Salami .... 59¢ ea

Sliced
BEEF LIVER .... 79¢ lb.

Bone-in
ROUND STEAK .... $1.16 lb.

TURKEY DRUMSTICKS ... 39¢ lb.

WHOLE FRYERS .... 49¢ lb.
(Cut-Up .... 59¢ lb.)

Boneless
RUMP ROAST .... $1.39 lb.

Boneless
SIRLOIN TIP STEAK .... $1.79 lb.

Boneless
SIRLOIN TIP ROAST .... $1.45 lb.

Less than 22% Fat, Lean
GROUND BEEF .... 99¢ lb.

---

preparation

You will want to obtain the following:

1. Grocery ads from your local newspapers— approximately fifteen different advertisements can be used.
2. Basic food groups chart—such as the one supplied by the National Dairy Council.

Guidelines to accompany the chart should also note the daily servings that each person should consume: meat group, 2 or more; milk group, 3 or more; vegetable and fruits group, 4 or more; and the bread and cereal group, 4 or more.

3. Calorie chart—to indicate the calorie ratings per serving amount for most commonly eaten foods.
4. Restaurant menus—such as those from Sambo's, Denny's, or any local restaurant. Some of the chain restaurants will give away their old menus every month or two when they bring out their new ones.

directions

As a beginning step, compare the grocery advertisement specials from several food markets. For example, if Sammy's Store is selling bacon for $1.19 a pound and the Lathrop Market has a 12-oz. package for 95¢, which is less expensive? With a hand-held calculator, it can quickly be determined that $1.19 ÷ 16 oz. = $.074 per oz., and $.95 ÷ 12 oz. = $.079 per oz. To continue with this type of unit pricing, devise a standard grocery list and have the students compare the advertisements from three or four markets to see which store would have the best total price. Also, determine how much more might have been saved by shopping for the specials at all of the stores. Finally, take one more step and go with the students to several markets—again with standard grocery lists—and record sizes and prices so that unit prices can again be determined.

Another worthwhile procedure is to set up a menu for one week (or one month) so that all family members will receive balanced diets.

*Weekly Menu**							
breakfast							
lunch							
dinner							
	sun.	mon.	tues.	wed.	thurs.	fri.	sat.

*Each person should have at least this many servings per day:
(A) 3 servings — milk group (milk, cheese, ice cream, etc.)
(B) 2 servings — meat group (meat, poultry, eggs, cheese with dry beans, etc.)
(C) 4 servings — vegetables and fruit (dark green or yellow vegetables, citrus fruit or tomatoes)
(D) 4 servings — breads and cereals (whole grain breads, cooked cereal, cornmeal, spaghetti, etc.)

That is, each family member should have at least a minimum number of servings from each food group each day—milk, meat, vegetables and fruit, and the bread and cereal groups. A chart, similar to the one illustrated, may help to organize such a diet.

A further extension of the weekly menu would be to determine how many calories an individual would be consuming on the proposed diet as compared to the recommended intake.

All of this, of course, could be related back to food costs and even to a family budget.

If the costs of meals at home (from the weekly menu) are determined, it is interesting to see what the cost of the same (or nearly the same) meal is at a restaurant. This can readily be determined by comparing the home meal costs with the menu prices for several restaurants. When doing so, don't forget the tax and service tip.

WRITE YOUR OWN
calculator problems
(grades 5–8)

purposes

To encourage students to write problems that relate to their own everyday lives

To allow students to utilize calculators for very large- or very small-number calculations

preparation

Have available a random assortment of reference materials (almanacs, etc.), perhaps interesting pictures or objects, and index cards for student use. Also, ask students to bring their own reference items—anything from baseball cards to a pet hamster, or a lucky charm.

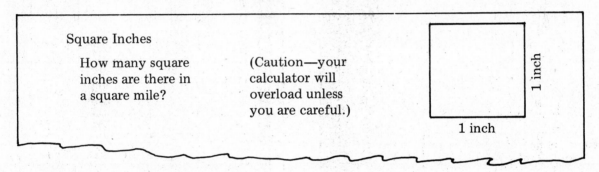

Square Inches

How many square inches are there in a square mile?

(Caution—your calculator will overload unless you are careful.)

1 inch

1 inch

directions

Tell the students that you wish to have them make up their own problems and write them on the index cards. Also, encourage them to use the reference materials or objects and the hand-held calculators to devise interesting problems with very large or very small numbers. You may also want to work on one or two model problems with them. If desired, the format from a Strategy for Analyzing Word Problems (see Chapter IX) may be used as a guide for setting up individual problems.

Allow the students to use the reference materials freely, to work together, and to try their problems on each other. As they devise, criticize, and refine the problems that they have written themselves, they will gain further understanding of how mathematics relates to many things in our everyday lives. Selected problems, followed by their answers, are noted below:

Baseball

Tickets to the baseball game cost $1.50. What will it cost a family of six to attend the game?

(Solution: 6 × $1.50 = $9.00)

Savings

The Savings and Loan Association where you have a savings account advertises daily interest. If you have $213.00 in you account at $5\frac{3}{4}\%$, how much interest will you receive each day?

(Solution: Daily interest is 5.75% ÷ 365 days = .01575% daily interest; then .01575% in decimal form is 0.0001575; thus, $213.00 × 0.0001575 = $.0335475, or you will receive about $3\frac{1}{3}$¢ of interest per day.)

CHAPTER XI

MEASUREMENT

By the time children first come to school they have likely learned to make direct measurement comparisons between objects. That is, they would probably realize that the teacher is taller than they are, the bucket will hold more water than the glass, a shoe is heavier than a crayon, etc. Their first directed measurement learning activities should then be to compare objects with nonstandard units. For example, they might determine how many hands long the teacher's desk is, how many glasses of water will fill the bucket, whether the indoor or the outdoor temperature is warmer, etc. The students should then be helped to understand that we may use nonstandard units to provide "rough" comparisons or equivalents, but that such measurements are not exact enough for many situations.

Measurement activities with standard units should be brought to students' attention next. Since the first of such activities will likely deal with length measurement, it is suggested that the paper clip (see Developing Measurement Standards with Paper Clips) serve as the initial standard. After utilizing paper clip measurement standards, the next step would be to focus on either the English or the metric (SI) system of measurement. However, since the United States is moving toward joining the rest of the world in the use of the metric system, the major emphasis in this chapter will be to set forth the basic elements of the metric system (see Learning Everyday Metric Measurement) and a series of related practice activities.

The third activity discussed in this chapter, Metric Treasure, suggests a procedure by which the students may determine the extent to which metric measures are already being used at home and in other facets of their daily lives. The next four activities—Measure My House, Measure Yourself Metrically,

Measurement Madness, and Go Fly a Paper Airplane—will provide varying types of linear measurement practice. These are followed by Take Me to Your Litre and Metric Capacity "Crossups" which focus upon metric volume/capacity measures. Then Weighing Rocks, Give a Gram, Get a Kilogram, and The Kilogram "Kracker" deal with the measurement of metric mass/weight. Recording Everyday Temperatures provides for the reading and recording of Celsius or Centigrade temperatures and Some Metric Recipes utilize metric measurements of several types.

Certain activities from other chapters in this book may also be modified for use as measurement exercises. Some of these are Box Puzzles in Chapter I, Straw Trading from Chapter II, Constructing 3 X 3 Magic Squares in Chapter III, Math Jigsaw Puzzles and Punch-Out Figures in Chapter IV, Scramble and Checkerboard Math from Chapter VIII, Mathematics Problem Solving in Everyday Life from Chapter IX, Classroom Uses for Hand-Held Calculators in Chapter X, and Constructing and Using a Hypsometer from Chapter XII.

developing MEASUREMENT standards with paper clips

(grades k–8)

purposes

To provide children with concrete measurement experiences

To help students develop an understanding of standard measurements

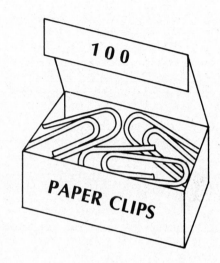

preparation

Obtain several boxes of the same size paper clips, a ball of string, and scissors. The students may also use pencils and paper for certain portions of the activities.

directions

Ask your students to guess (estimate) how many hands long the teacher's desk is. As soon as they have made a guess (upper-grade students should record this estimate), allow them to actually measure it with their hands. Continue this procedure by measuring other objects such as the chalkboard height, width of the room, etc., until their guesses are about the same as their actual hand measurements. Then, pick one item, such as one student's height, that everyone is to measure with their hands. After measuring, ask each of them to use their hand measurements to cut a length of string that is exactly as tall as the student they measured. Hang all of the strings from a standard position, perhaps the top of the chalkboard, and notice that the strings vary in length. Then ask why, since they all measured the height of the same student, the strings are not the same length. Undoubtedly, someone will volunteer that their hands are not of the same size. At this point, discuss with them the need for having everyone use something of the same size (standard measuring device) to measure with.

Distribute paper clips to each of the students and ask them to compare them to see whether they are standard in length. Once they have determined that the paper clips are uniform, suggest that they all estimate the number of paper clips a certain object is, such as the width of a student desk, and then carefully lay paper clips end to end and find a precise measurement. If the task is completed with care, each student will determine the same paper clip measurement. Thus, they may conclude that paper clips are a much more accurate standard measuring tool than the hands of individual students.

Once the students have become quite proficient at estimating and measuring with standard size paper clips, challenge them with a more difficult problem such as how many paper clips there are from a table top to the floor. Since they cannot line up their paper clips end to end as before, they must determine another process. Very soon some student will decide to make a paper clip chain, and then the solution is easily determined.

171

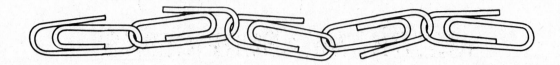

Paper clip chains may be of any length, but I suggest that the students make them in segments of ten (10, 20, 30 . . . 100), and that a piece of string be attached to every tenth clip to allow counting by 10s rather than by 1s each time. Then, have them use the paper clip chain to estimate and measure numerous things such as window sizes, room width, length of the playground, etc.

As described above, paper clips can become one of the first standard measuring objects to be handled by young children. They can also be used in the same manner by older students, to reinforce the use of and the need for measuring standards, without having to deal with the specifics of either the English or metric systems.

By using standard measurement devices, such as paper clips, a natural "lead-in" to the use of predominant measurement systems occurs. Thus, a study of either the metric or the English system should follow. It appears that the United States will soon be adopting metric measurement as its major system. Thus, most of the measurement activities that follow will be discussed metrically. However, with slight modifications, many of them could also be used for reinforcing English measurement.

Learning everyday
METRIC MEASUREMENTS

(grades k–8)

purposes

To provide students with pertinent examples of linear (length), capacity (volume), mass (weight), and temperature measurements in the metric system

To help students to become familiar with metric prefixes and symbols

preparation

You will want to procure or construct the following metric equipment:

1. metre tape
2. centimetre ruler
3. litre container
4. millilitre beaker
5. 1 gram to 1,000 gram mass pieces and a pan balance (or a spring scale that can weigh items to 1,000 grams)
6. Celsius (centigrade) thermometer

directions

As the students, and you, work on becoming familiar with the SI (Système International) Metric System, which has been adopted by the United States, it may be helpful to refer to the following chart.

	Linear (length)	Capacity (volume)	Mass (weight)
1,000 kilo (k)			
100 hecto (h)			
10 deka (da)			
1 (base unit)	metre (m)	litre (l)	gram (g)
.1 deci (d)			
.01 centi (c)			
.001 milli (m)			

As students work with the metric system, they will soon determine that a prefix attached to a base unit gives it a specific power of 10 value. For example, if kilo is attached to metre, we have kilometre which means 1,000 metres.

Also, if centi and metre are combined, the result is a centimetre or .01 of a metre in length. The same procedure is also utilized for capacity and mass measurements, such that a dekalitre would refer to 10 litres and a milligram means

173

.001 of a gram.

The chart can further be utilized to derive the symbols for the commonly used metric measurements. Note that the h from hecto when attached to the m from metre becomes hm which means hectometre or 100 metres. Likewise, when the m from milli and the l from litre are put together, we have ml which means .001 of a litre. Please remember that these are sym- bols and, as such, no periods follow them. Also, an *s* is never used with a metric symbol; for example, 6 kg stands for 6 kilograms.

The chart will become much more meaningful after the students, and you, have had direct experiences with metric measurement devices and activities. Thus, a brief look at each of the metric measurement systems for everyday use is provided below:

1. *Metric Linear (length) Measurement*

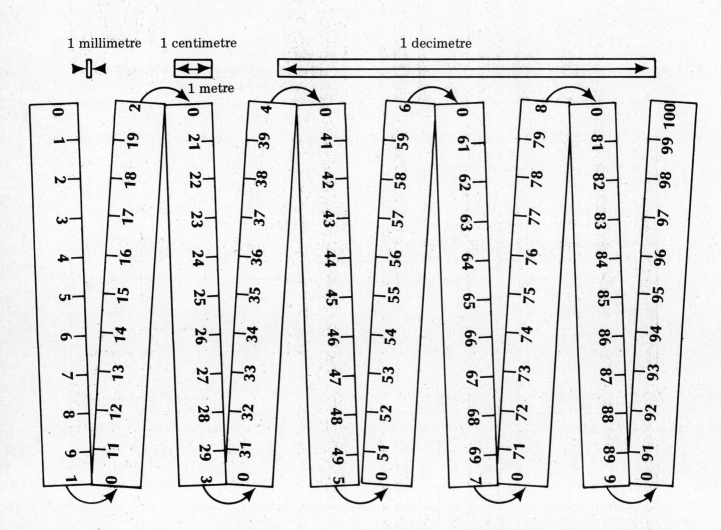

*A Metre Tape and a Centimetre Ruler for classroom reproduction purposes are located in Appendix B, Item 17.

Length measurement activities generally begin with the metre. Young students may learn to relate to it as slightly taller (or shorter) than they are. During second or third grade, the students can generally begin to work with shorter and longer segments of the metre. They will eventually need to readily identify the following metric linear measurements (those used most frequently in daily life are underlined):

kilometre	(km)	=	1,000 metres
hectometre	(hm)	=	100 metres
dekametre	(dam)	=	10 metres
metre	(m)	=	1 metre
decimetre	(dm)	=	.1 metre
centimetre	(cm)	=	.01 metre
millimetre	(mm)	=	.001 metre

As the students become more adept, they should be able to accurately measure a variety of distances. The teacher might also ask them to identify specific positions on a metric ruler such as the following:

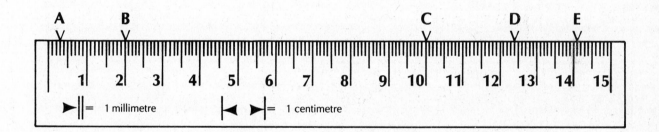

Point A indicates 3 mm, B is at 20 mm or 2 cm, C shows 100 mm or 10 cm or 1 dm, D equals 124 mm or 12.4 cm or 1.24 dm, and E points to 141 mm or 14.1 cm or 1.41 dm. In each instance the preferred manner for relating the measurements is underlined.

To become proficient with linear metric measurement, it is necessary to practice these skills on a periodic basis. Thus, other length measurement activities are described in four later sections of this chapter. They are Measure My House, Measure Yourself Metrically, Measurement Madness, and Go Fly a Paper Airplane.

2. *Metric Capacity (volume) Measurement*

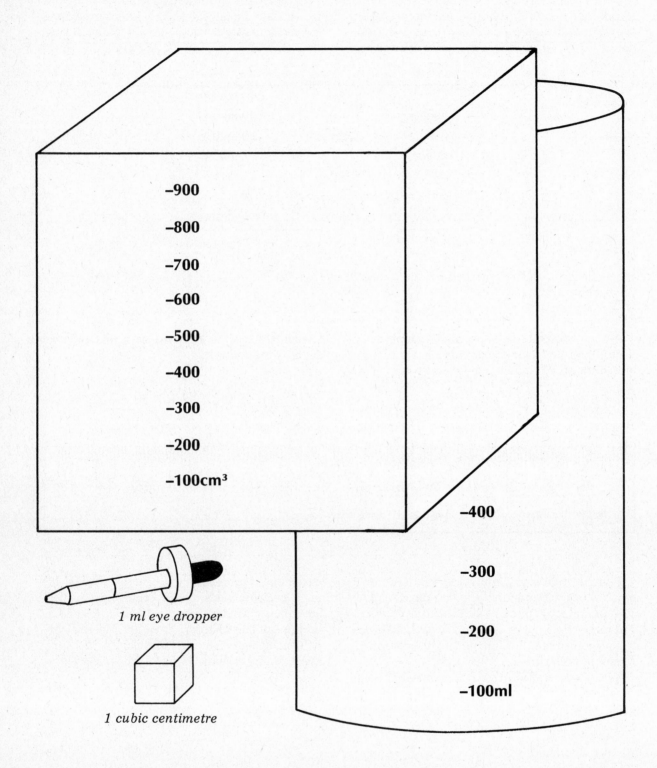

–900

–800

–700

–600

–500

–400

–300

–200

–100cm³

–400

–300

–200

–100ml

1 ml eye dropper

1 cubic centimetre

Metric capacity measurement is generally set forth according to a cube that measures 1 decimetre on a side (see illustration). Such a cube measures 1 dm × 1 dm × 1 dm = 1 dm³ or, since 1 dm = 10 cm, 10 cm × 10 cm × 10 cm = 1,000 cm³ (stated as 1,000 cubic centimetres). The same amount of liquid that it takes to fill a cubic decimetre container will also exactly fill a litre container (see illustration). Thus, a cubic decimetre will hold the same volume (capacity) as a litre. For everyday measurements, the litre, and its multiples and subparts, are most commonly used. The following chart may help to explain how the litre and dm³, as well as their subparts and multiples, are related (also, the units used most frequently in everyday life are underlined):

kilolitre	(kl)	=	1,000 litres
hectolitre	(hl)	=	100 litres
dekalitre	(dal)	=	10 litres
litre	(l)	=	1 litre
decilitre	(dl)	=	.1 litre
centilitre	(cl)	=	.01 litre
millilitre	(ml)	=	.001 litre

Young students may pour water from the cubic decimetre into litre containers of several different shapes in order that they may begin to develop a concept of how much a litre is. Older students should relate portions of a litre in terms of millilitres and decimal parts of a litre. For example, a litre container filled one-half full should be called 500 ml or .5 litre. The best way to practice these skills is to pour various amounts of water into litre and millilitre containers and to have the students state the amounts as precisely as possible.

If your budget allows, you may purchase scientific-type litre and millilitre beakers from an educational supplier. However, they can also be acquired quite inexpensively by simply purchasing litre and 500 ml bottles of soda pop (Coke, 7-UP, Shasta, Pepsi, etc.). The soda bottles can then be marked in 100 millilitre divisions with a permanent marking pen. Also, extra 1 millilitre (or 1 cubic centimetre = 1 cc) eye or ear droppers can be found in many home medicine chests.

It is also possible to construct litre and millilitre containers from ½ gallon milk cartons. The inside length and width of such cartons is generally 9.5 cm × 9.5 cm. Thus, if the carton is cut off at an approximate height of 11.1 cm (you may wish to cut it off at 12 cm and notch

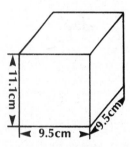

the corner for a pouring spout to an inside height of 11.1 cm), it will hold 1 litre. Capacity containers of less than a litre can be made from additional milk containers by simply allowing approximately 1.11 cm in height for each 100 ml of volume.

As soon as the students have developed a basic understanding of litres and millilitres, and they are able to properly record their results with pencil and paper, they should be challenged further. Several possibilities would include prescribing the activities Metric Treasure, Metric Capacity "Crossups," Take Me to Your Litre, and Some Metric Recipes, which are found later in this chapter.

3. *Metric Mass (weight) Measurement*

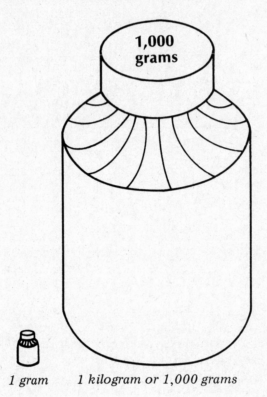

1 gram   1 kilogram or 1,000 grams

Metric mass measurements begin with the gram. A gram has about the same weight as 1 raisin. However, for everyday measurements you will more frequently deal with the kilogram (about 2.2 pounds) which equals 1,000 grams. (For reference purposes, a litre of water has a mass of 1 kilogram.) The following chart, with the terms most frequently used in everyday life underlined, may help to set forth the metric system for mass measurement:

kilogram	(kg)	=	1,000 grams
hectogram	(hg)	=	100 grams
dekagram	(dag)	=	10 grams
gram	(g)	=	1 gram
decigram	(dg)	=	.1 gram
centigram	(cg)	=	.01 gram
milligram	(mg)	=	.001 gram

The terms *mass* and *weight* are commonly used to mean the same thing. Technically, however, mass refers to the amount of matter in a physical body whereas weight is dependent upon gravitational pull. Here on earth, for all practical purposes, they are the same; but if you were on the moon, your mass would remain constant while your weight would register considerably less. However, when working with elementary students no great difficulty will be encountered if we talk of finding someone's weight rather than his mass.

Possibly the best way to begin acquainting young students with metric weight (mass) is to have them try to find objects that weigh a gram and a kilogram. For example, a small paper clip or a raisin will weigh about a gram each, and a large dictionary might have a mass of 1,000 grams or 1 kilogram.

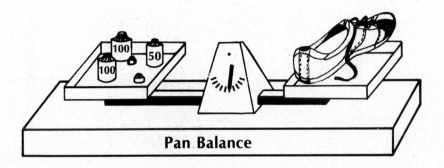

Pan Balance

A two-pan balance together with a set of 1 to 1,000 gram mass pieces can be excellent learning tools when dealing with the metric weight of objects. For example, a student's shoe might be placed in one of the pans and mass pieces to counterbalance it in seesaw fashion in the other. When balanced, the gram amounts for all mass pieces are added together to equal the weight of the shoe—the shoe illustrated weighs 256 grams.

Upper-grade students may also accomplish mass measurements with pan scales, or they may utilize spring scales to weigh a variety of items. Of particular interest at this level is determining one's own body mass. As such, a metric bathroom scale may show a student to weigh 40 kg (approximately 88 pounds). One further point of interest for upper-grade students might be the metric tonne (T) which is equivalent to 1,000 kilograms.

If students are to learn and retain concepts relating to metric weight (mass), they must be exposed to them repeatedly. In addition to locating everyday items that display metric weights, three activities that students find interesting are located in later sections of this chapter. They are Weighing Rocks, Kilogram "Kracker," and Some Metric Recipes.

4. *Relationships between Metric Length, Capacity, and Mass Measurements*

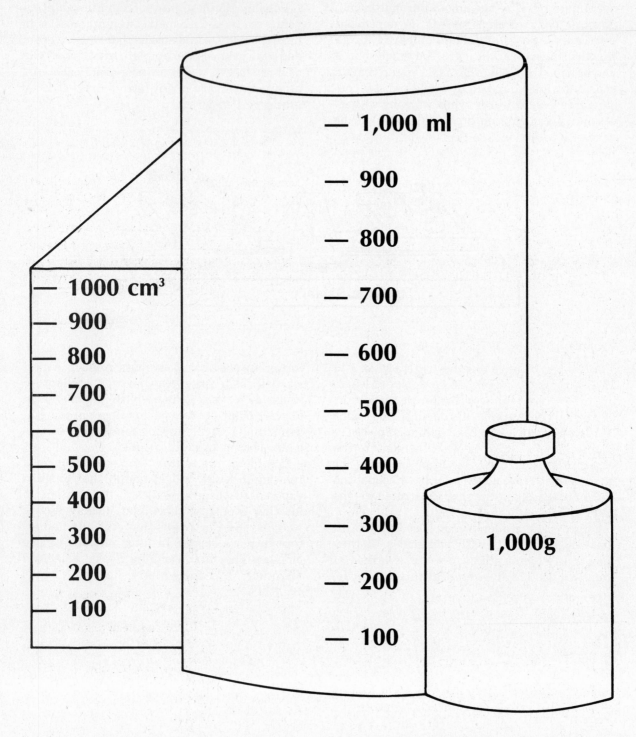

The metric units for length, capacity, and mass share a relationship that is commonly expressed in one of two formats.

One of the representations (see dm³ = l = kg illustration) notes that cubic decimetre and litre containers hold the same volume. Furthermore, when either is filled with water (under specific conditions, otherwise slight variations will occur), that water will weigh a kilogram. Noting the relationship in a second format (see cm³ = ml = g illustration), we find that the

capacity of a cubic centimetre and a millilitre are the same. In addition, the weight of an amount of water required to fill either is one gram.

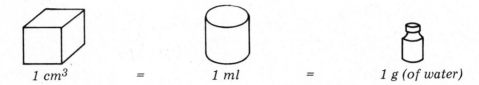

1 cm³   =   1 ml   =   1 g (of water)

When comparing the two representations, notice that the dm³ = 1,000 cm³, the l = 1,000 ml, and the kg = 1,000 g. Thus, they actually represent the same relationship with one being 1,000 times larger (or smaller) than the other.

In order for students to master these related concepts, they may first pour water from the

decimetre cube into the litre container to determine that they have the same volume. Then, after offsetting the weight of the empty container, they should use a two-pan scale to compare the weight of a litre of water with that of a kilogram mass piece. The result will be, of course, that they have exactly the same weight.

5. *Metric Temperature Measurement*

Under the metric system everyday thermometer readings will be related according to the Celsius, or centigrade, temperature scale. Celsius was the name of the person who devised the centigrade thermometer scale; thus, today we usually talk of temperature in degrees Celsius (°C).

As can be seen in the illustration, water freezes at 0°C and boils at 100°C. While most other temperatures that concern us are between these two points, it may also prove helpful to be aware of the following cooking and food preservation temperatures:

270°C — Broil
230°C — Hot oven
180°C — Moderate oven
130°C — Warm oven
5°C — Refrigerator
–20°C — Freezer

To help students to become familiar with Celsius temperatures, have them do simple experiments with thermometers. Keep track of daily temperatures and have them record their

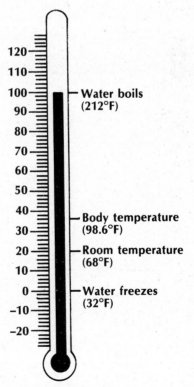

Celsius thermometer

findings on duplicated thermometer diagrams (see Appendix B, Item 28). Let them determine their body temperatures. With a dipping thermometer find the Celsius temperatures of running hot and cold tap water. Put a thermometer in a refrigerator or a freezer and read the temperature after ten minutes. You may even want to do some classroom cooking that utilizes Celsius temperatures (and other metric measures). For these purposes, two sections titled Recording Everyday Temperatures and Some Metric Recipes are found later in this chapter.

METRIC TREASURE

(grades 1–8)

purpose

To become familiar with items from daily life that are measured metrically

preparation

Bring two or three products to school that have been marked metrically. Also, reproduce a worksheet similar to the one illustrated.

directions

After students have mastered basic concepts relating to metric length, volume, weight, and temperature, challenge them to find metric items from their homes and community. Show them where several items are marked metrically. For example, a bar of soap may have its weight listed in grams, a container of medicine may have a volume in millilitres, etc. Then distribute duplicated copies of the worksheet and ask that they search their homes (and community) that afternoon for metrically marked items. They should record the products located together with the measurements and come to school the next day ready to tell about their findings. If it is feasible, they may also bring the products to school for display purposes. Finally, if a scoring procedure will help to motivate the students, one scheme for assigning points is shown on the worksheet.

METRIC TREASURE

Name _____

Look in your mother's cupboards, on grocery store shelves, or in other places to find five things that are measured metrically. Write the name of the product and its metric measurement.

Product	Measurement
_____	_____
_____	_____
_____	_____
_____	_____
_____	_____

Scoring (optional): The point values for different items are:

5 points for a cereal or food product
4 points for soap or cleaning product
3 points for medicine
2 points for measuring devices (diet scales, measuring cups, metre sticks, etc.)
1 point for any other items

Rank:

25 points—very good (Superstar)
24–15 points—good (Star)
14–10 points—fair (Ranger)
 9–4 points—keep trying (Searcher)
 3–0 points—open your eyes (Sleeper)

*See Appendix B, Item 18, for an enlarged Metric Treasure worksheet.

MEASURE MY HOUSE

(grades 1–4)

purpose

To provide practice with measuring metric lengths to the nearest centimetre

preparation

The students will need centimetre rulers, Measure My House worksheets, and pencils.

directions

Ask the students to measure the height of the door to the closest whole centimetre. Be certain that each student is reading the measurement from his ruler correctly. As soon as everyone has succeeded, record the answer and try another measurement such as the width of the house, etc. Then have them measure and record various other house measurement questions (samples are listed on the worksheet in Appendix B).

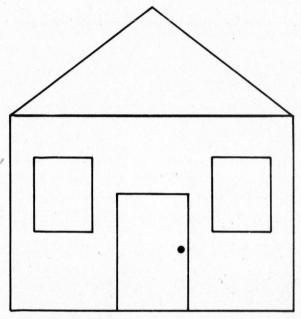

*See Appendix B, Item 19, for an enlarged Measure My House worksheet.

variations

A number of figures might be designed by the teacher and duplicated for student measurement purposes. For example, a dog drawing might be measured from the nose to the tip of its tail, a fire engine from bumper to bumper, etc.

As the students become more adept, they might take such measurements to the nearest millimetre. Also, such exercises might be used with English measurements to the nearest inch, 1/2 inch, or 1/16 inch.

MEASURE yourself METRICALLY

(grades 2–8)

purposes

To provide metric length measurement practice

To determine each student's individual metric measurements

preparation

The students will need metric tape measures (see Appendix B, Item 17, for a paper metre tape that they can construct), pencils, and the Measure Yourself Metrically worksheet (see Appendix B, Item 20).

directions

Begin by having the students work together to find their individual metre heights to the nearest centimetre. Once they have done this correctly, have them estimate their waist size, record it, and then use a metre tape to measure it. Using the same process, have them estimate and then measure to determine other body part measures. They might measure the length of an arm or leg, their hat or head size, the width of their widest smile, etc.

variations

The same procedure could easily be utilized for U.S. customary or English measurements. In such instances the students would need to estimate and measure to the nearest inch, or foot and inch.

*See Appendix B, Item 20, for a reproducible worksheet to accompany this task.

MEASUREMENT MAdNESS

(grades 3–8)

purposes

To reinforce metric linear measurement concepts by drawing lines of specified lengths

To introduce an element of chance

preparation

Each student will need a centimetre ruler, a pencil, and a Measurement Madness worksheet. The teacher will need a chalkboard spinner (see Chapter VIII) or a pair of dice.

directions

Measurement Madness is played by drawing a series of straight lines that begin at the Start X (see illustration) and are attached end to end in an effort to have those lines end within figures A, B, C, D, and E in order. The length of each succeeding line is determined each time the teacher spins the spinner (or rolls dice) to indicate cm lengths. The only restriction is that the lines must remain on the paper. To provide further clarification, a sample game for two players is illustrated below.

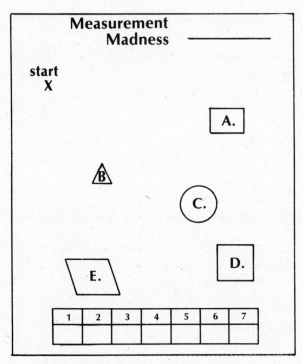

*See Appendix B, Item 21, for an enlarged Measurement Madness worksheet.

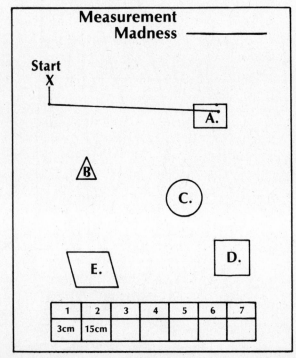

Player 1

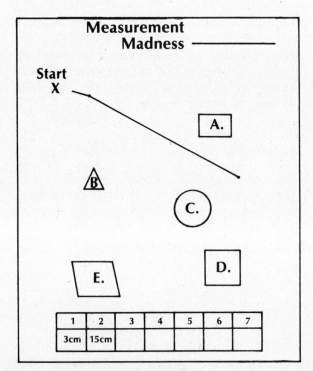

Player 2

The game started with the chalkboard spinner pointing to 3 cm. Each player then recorded the amount of this first spin in the space provided at the bottom of the page and drew a line of that length from her own Start X. However, since a 3 cm line could not reach Figure A, Player 1 sketched hers downward whereas Player 2 drew hers directly toward Figure A. The next spin yielded 15 cm and Player 1 drew her 15 cm line, from the end of the prior 3 cm line, and was able to end within Figure A. She will now be able to try for Figure B. Player 2, however, could not end within Figure A and therefore chose to draw her 15 cm line off at an angle. Thus, she will have to try for Figure A again on her next turn. The game continues in this manner with the winner being the first person to end within Figure E, or the one who has accomplished ending within the most figures in proper order at the end of a specified time.

variations

Measurement Madness could be played with chalkboard spinner units like .001 m, .001 hm, and 152 mm if the students are quite adept with metrics and they need to be challenged. Another variation involves playing the game on the playground with selected locations being designated as areas A, B, C, D, and E. In this instance the spinner numerals might read as 1 dam, 7 m, 13.2 m, and .005 km.

The Measurement Madness activity can also be readily adapted for use with inches, feet, yards, and even miles. However, keep in mind that converting between these units can be difficult.

Go Fly a Paper Airplane

(grades 4–8)

purposes

To provide interesting metric measurement practice

To begin utilizing metric measurement in an applied situation

preparation

The students will need the Go Fly a Paper Airplane worksheet, assorted size sheets of paper, and a metre stick.

directions

Ask your students to tell what makes a paper airplane fly. Solicit the idea that different designs may fly better than others and then suggest that for today's mathematics lesson they will be able to make and fly their own paper airplanes. Next distribute the Go Fly a Paper Airplane worksheets and discuss the measurements that they will need to make—length, width, depth, area, perimeter, etc. Then bring out the assorted sheets of paper and the metre sticks. As soon as they have selected a sheet of paper, let them begin work. The teacher may need to provide assistance or check on the accuracy of measurements, but for the most part the students will happily complete the tasks on their own. There will be, of course, a bit of competition when it comes to determining which plane will fly the greatest distance.

variation

Go Fly a Paper Airplane is a task that might readily be adapted for use with English system measurements. As such, the measurements would be made to the nearest inch, foot, and yard.

Go Fly a Paper Airplane

Task A—Measure the following with a metre stick:
1. Length of starting paper = _____
2. Width of starting paper = _____

Task B—Make your favorite design of paper airplane and measure:
1. Length of the plane = _____
2. Width at the tail = _____
3. Depth at the tail = _____

Bonus:
1. What is the area of the paper? _____
2. What is the perimeter? _____
3. What is the greatest distance your airplane will fly? _____

*See Appendix B, Item 22, for an enlarged Go Fly a Paper Airplane worksheet.

TAKE ME TO YOUR LITRE
(grades 3–8)

purposes

To manipulate various millilitre amounts of water up to 1 litre

To provide interesting practice with metric volume measurements

preparation

The materials needed are:

1. one large pail able to hold about 5 litres of water
2. one small cup (used to take water from the pail)
3. two to four litre containers (which each player will try to fill)
4. one 100-millilitre graduated cylinder
5. one Take Me to Your Litre gameboard
6. two different colored dice
7. two to four different markers (to be moved on the gameboard)

*A complete Take Me to Your Litre gameboard for classroom use is found in Appendix B, Item 23.

directions

Each of the two to four players, in turn, begins with his marker in the Start Here box. To move, the dice are thrown and the numbers which come up tell the player how many spaces he must move; for example, if the red die shows 1 and the blue die indicates 2 he moves his marker to the square that says "Take 90 ml" (see illustration). He then performs the required task on that square; in this instance he pours 90 ml of water into his litre container. Play progresses in this manner with the players taking turns. If a square landed on has no directions, then the player neither adds nor loses water on that turn. If a player comes to the edge of the gameboard before he has moved the required number of spaces, he must "rebound" and go in the opposite direction; for example, if the blue die shows 6, but he has only 2 spaces remaining in the upward direction, he must move those 2 spaces up and "rebound" four spaces back down in the same column. The first player to obtain 1 litre of water, or more, is declared the winner.

METRIC CAPACITY "CROSSUPS"

(grades 4–8)

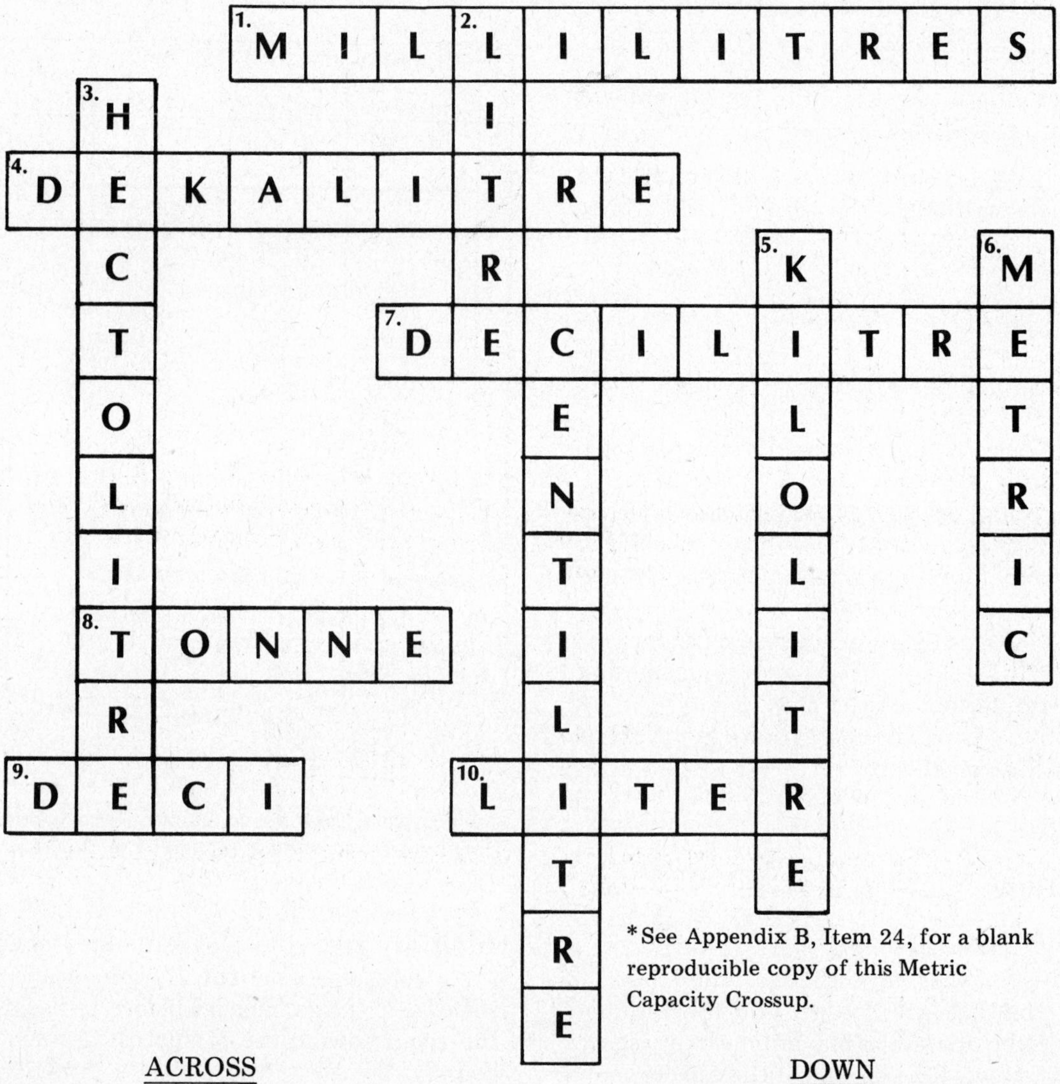
1. MILLILITRES
2. LITRE
3. HECTOLITRE
4. DEKALITRE
5. KILOLITRE
6. METRIC
7. DECILITRE
8. TONNE
9. DECI
10. LITER
CENTILITRE

*See Appendix B, Item 24, for a blank reproducible copy of this Metric Capacity Crossup.

<u>ACROSS</u>

1. 1,000 ________ = 1 litre.
4. A large pail might hold a ________.
7. $\frac{1}{10}$ of a litre = ________.
8. 1,000 litres of water would weigh a metric ________.
9. The prefix ________ means .1.
10. Sometimes you may find litre spelled as ________.

<u>DOWN</u>

2. 1,000 ml = 1 ________.
3. 100 litres = ________.
5. 1,000 litres = ________.
6. Litres, metres, and grams are ________ units of measure.

purpose

To reinforce concepts relating to metric capacity (volume) and prefix meanings

preparation

Each student will need a blank Metric Capacity "Crossup" worksheet (see Appendix B, Item 24) and a pencil. It would also be helpful to have the various sizes of metric containers at some location in the classroom so that students could look at them (or even experiment with water) as they seek the "crossup" answers.

directions

You may wish to utilize different sizes of metric volume containers as you review the meanings of the prefixes with your students. Then distribute duplicated copies of a Metric Capacity "Crossup" to them and complete one answer with them. As soon as some of the students have completed the "crossup," check their answers and then have them help others who are having more difficulty. If particular questions cause difficulty consistently, take time out to discuss or demonstrate how a particular result was achieved.

variations

If some of your students are very adept at "crossups," challenge them to create their own. Give them centimetre graph paper and illustrate how the words cross at a common letter. Then, when they have a series of crossed metric words, explain how to number them and write questions for each. A blank numbered grid, together with the questions, should be set up on a second sheet of graph paper. Finally, let them exchange with another student and then try to solve each other's Metric "Crossups."

WEIGHING ROCKS

(grades 3–8)

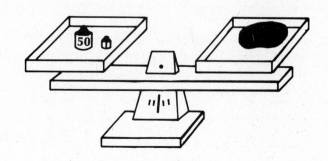

purposes

To estimate metric weight (mass) by manipulating rocks of various sizes

To provide interesting practice with metric weight measurements

preparation

A two-pan balance scale together with a set of 1 to 1,000 gram mass pieces or a spring scale that has at least a 2 kilogram capacity will be needed. Also, a Weighing Rocks worksheet is provided in Appendix B, Item 25.

directions

Ask each of the students to bring a rock to the classroom that is about the size of a large marble. Then ask them to estimate how many grams it weighs. To do so, they may hold gram mass pieces in one hand and their rock in the other. After they have completed their estimates, put each rock on the pan balance (or spring scale) and counterbalance it with mass pieces (see illustration). Then ask how close their estimate was to the actual weight.

For the next day's assignment, have them bring in a rock about the size of a baseball. Set all of the rocks on a table and ask them to see which weighs the closest to a kilogram. Then check their estimates with a scale.

Further, have each student bring in five rocks. Ask them to see if they can find a rock that weighs 1 gram and to estimate the weights of each of the other rocks. The chart below may help to organize their data.

Rock	1	2	3	4	5
Estimate					
Weight					
Difference					

*See Appendix B, Item 25, for the Weighing Rocks worksheet that includes a chart of this type.

variation

The Weighing Rocks activity can easily be adapted for use with U.S. customary weight measurements. All that is needed is a scale that indicates pounds and ounces.

GIVE A GRAM, GET A kilogram

(grades 4–8)

purposes

To manipulate various gram weights up to a kilogram

To provide interesting practice with metric mass (weight) measurements

preparation

The materials needed are:

1. one complete set of 1 to 1,000 gram mass pieces
2. one two-pan balance scale
3. one Give a Gram, Get a Kilogram game-board
4. two different colored dice
5. two to four different markers (to be moved on the gameboard)
6. pencils and paper

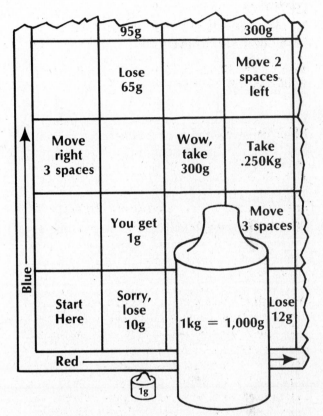

* A complete Give a Gram, Get a Kilogram gameboard is found in Appendix B, Item 26.

directions

From two to four students may play Give a Gram, Get a Kilogram. Each player, at her turn, puts her marker in the Start Here box. She then rolls the dice, and the numbers which come up tell the player how many spaces to move; for example, if both the red and the blue dice come up showing 2 then the player moves her marker to the square that says "Wow, take 300 g" (see illustration). She then keeps track of her Get a Kilogram score by recording the 300 g on her sheet of paper. With each turn the players add to or subtract from their Get a Kilogram score; however, they cannot obtain a score of less than 0 grams. If a square landed on has no directions the player neither adds nor loses weight on that turn. If a player comes to the edge of the gameboard before she has

moved the required number of spaces, she must "rebound" and go in the opposite direction; for example, if the red die shows 5, but she has only 3 spaces to the right remaining, she must move those 3 spaces to the right and then "rebound" 2 spaces left in the same row.

The first player to obtain at least 1 kilogram (1,000 grams) may be declared the winner; however, she must "prove" that she did in fact Get a Kilogram. To do so, she must set the kilogram mass piece on one side of the two-pan balance and add to or subtract from the other side of the pan scale in the same order as she made weight scores on the gameboard. If her calculations were correct, and if she did, in fact, Get a Kilogram, she is declared the winner.

193

THE kilogRAM "kRACkER"

(grades 4–8)

purposes

To estimate the weight (mass) of everyday items in terms of kilograms

To manipulate and determine the precise weights of objects

preparation

You will need a metric scale or pan balance with a capacity of at least 2 kilograms. In addition, a random assortment of items, for estima-

tion and weighing purposes, will need to be gathered together.

directions

Ask the students to help gather items such as a pencil, ruler, scissors, stapler, etc. They should then estimate the weight of these items in relation to a kilogram. Do remind the students that 1,000 grams = 1 kilogram (or 1 gram = .001 kilogram) and allow them to handle the 1 to 1,000 gram mass pieces as they attempt to establish a manipulative concept for the various weights.

After each student has handled a particular

item, ask him to record the estimated weight of the particular object. Next, put the item on a scale and determine its actual weight in terms of a kilogram. For example, if the mass of a pencil was 23 grams it would be recorded as .023 kilograms. Further, the pencil's weight might also be recorded in terms of some other metric unit such as .23 hg or 23,000 mg. The chart below might help to organize such data.

Items to Weigh:

1. Pencil
2. Ruler
3. Scissors
4. Stapler
5. Something of your choice

	Estimate		Actual Weight in Kilograms		Weight in g, dag, hg, dg, cg, or mg	
1.	.015	kg	.023	kg	23	g
2.		kg		kg		dag
3.		kg		kg		mg
4.		kg		kg		cg
5.		kg		kg		dg

*See Appendix B, Item 27, for an enlarged Kilogram "Kracker" worksheet.

194

RECORDING EVERYDAY TEMPERATURES

(grades 1–8)

purposes

To help students learn to read and record Celsius (centigrade) temperatures

To begin to use Celsius temperatures in everyday situations

preparation

You will need at least one Celsius thermometer. However, several different types—indoor, outdoor, medical, dipping, oven, freezer (some can serve for several purposes)—of thermometers can be most helpful. Also, duplicated thermometer diagrams (see Appendix B, Item 28) can be of help to the students.

directions

When students are first exposed to Celsius thermometers, they will need to practice reading the temperatures. For example, Thermometer A in the illustration shows a normal room temperature. "What is its reading?" As they develop these understandings, the students should also be asked to record selected temperatures on thermometer diagrams (see Appendix B for thermometer diagrams).

Once the students are able to read and record temperatures, you may wish to arrange simple experiments for them. Such experiments or tasks might include:

1. *Daily outdoor temperatures.*

   At 9 o'clock each morning for a week read the Celsius thermometer and record the temperatures on the thermometer diagrams. "What were the highest and lowest temperatures this week?"

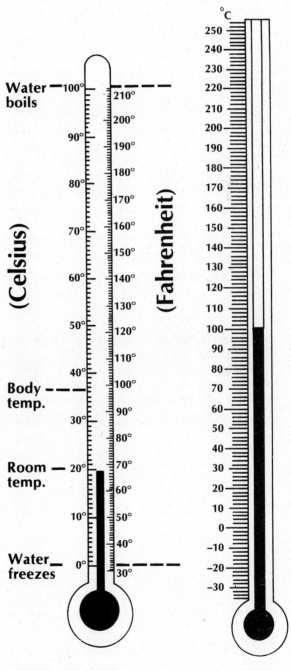

*See Appendix B, Item 28, for Celsius thermometer diagrams for classroom use.

2. *Hot and cold water temperatures.*

Use the dipping thermometer to find the Celsius temperatures of cold faucet water after 1 minute, 2 minutes, and 3 minutes. Then, in the same way, find the temperatures for hot water from a faucet. "What was the lowest cold water temperature?" "What was the highest Celsius reading for hot water?"

3. *Body temperature.*

Get the medical thermometer and clean it with alcohol. Then put the thermometer bulb under your tongue for 3 minutes. "What is your body temperature?"

Take another thermometer and place the bulb under your arm for 10 minutes. "What temperature did you find with this method?" (You should get the same body temperature reading in this way as you did when placing the other thermometer under your tongue.)

4. *Food-keeping temperatures.*

Find a thermometer that can be read in degrees below zero Celsius. Put that thermometer in a refrigerator (not the freezer section) for 15 minutes. Then read it quickly after opening the door, otherwise the temperature reading will go up again. "What was the refrigerator temperature?"

5. *Cooking temperatures.*

Put a Celsius oven thermometer into an oven and turn the oven dial to warm (approximately 270° F). Wait until the oven indicator shows that the proper temperature has been reached. Then, being careful not to touch the inside of the oven or the thermometer, take your first reading for a warm oven. "What Celsius temperature is a warm oven?" Repeat the same process for a moderate oven (360° F), a hot oven (450° F), and broiling (520° F). "What were the Celsius temperatures for each of these oven settings?"

In the event that you or the students should need to convert degrees Fahrenheit to degrees Celsius or the reverse, the formulas are:

$$°C = \frac{°F-32}{1.8} \qquad °F = (1.8 \times °C) + 32$$

Other tasks, such as calibrating a thermometer, could also be carried out with the students. However, if they have mastered the types of tasks set forth here they should encounter few difficulties with everyday metric temperatures.

SOME METRIC RECIPES

(grades k–8)

purposes

To use metric volume, weight, and temperature measurements in an applied setting

To eat and enjoy the results of metric measurement

preparation

You will want to have at hand the following items:

1. One 250 ml measuring cup (which is the same size as your "old" measuring cup).
2. A 5 ml teaspoon and a 15 ml tablespoon (which are the same sizes as the cooking teaspoons and tablespoons that you have previously been using).
3. A kitchen scale that shows gram weights.
4. A Celsius oven thermometer (unless the oven dial has dual markings for both Celsius and Fahrenheit temperatures; or, if necessary, you can convert from one temperature scale to the other by using the formulas from Recording Everyday Temperatures in the previous section of this chapter).

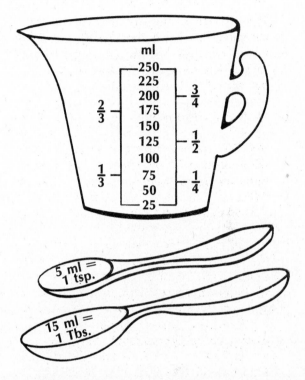

5. Finally, the kitchen utensils and the ingredients noted on the recipes must be available.

directions

Any number of recipes could be used metrically. However, three that are easily completed in a classroom setting are cited below. So go ahead and gather utensils, mix ingredients, cook where necessary, and then eat and enjoy.

Metric Punch

750 ml pineapple juice
125 ml lemon juice
125 ml sugar

250 ml cranberry juice
500 ml ginger ale
ice cubes

Put the ingredients into a large bowl, stir well, and serve.

Chewy Oatmeal Cookies

250 ml sifted all-purpose flour
3 g soda
3 g salt
2.5 g cinnamon
.5 g nutmeg
dash of cloves
175 ml shortening, soft

335 ml firmly packed brown sugar
2 eggs

5 ml vanilla
750 ml oats, uncooked
250 ml raisins
375 ml chopped walnut meats

Sift together flour, soda, salt, cloves, cinnamon, and nutmeg into bowl. Add shortening, sugar, eggs, and vanilla; beat until smooth—about 2 minutes. Stir in oats, raisins, and walnut meats. Drop by heaping teaspoonfuls onto greased cookie sheet. Bake in preheated moderate oven (175° C) for 12 to 15 minutes. Makes about 36 cookies.

Individual Blueberry Pancakes
30 ml Bisquick
5 ml egg (well beaten)
20 ml milk
5 ml blueberries

Pour ingredients into a bowl, stir for 2 minutes. Preheat the electric frying pan and pour 5 ml cooking oil into it. Pour the pancake batter into the pan. When bubbles are popping and leaving holes, turn your pancake over with a spatula. When bottom is brown, take it out and put it on a paper plate. Put butter and syrup on your pancake, and EAT.

CHAPTER XII

GEOMETRY

⊚◎◉◎◉◎◉◎◉◎◉◎◉◎

The applications of geometry in our everyday lives are many and varied. Geometric concepts are used in map reading, flower arrangements, scale drawings, building construction, and almost all commercially produced objects. Such concepts can also be found in many natural settings as circular tree trunks, flowers shaped as pentagons, parallel vein structures in plant stalks and leaves, etc. Thus, geometry should be seen as being important in helping students understand their environment. Furthermore, it should be studied in terms of geometric concepts that are useful to children and within their realm of understanding.

Beginning in kindergarten, children should learn the names and shapes of plane figures. The first three activities in this chapter—Sort the Shapes, Color a Geometric Picture, and Geometry Bean Bag Toss—will prove to be of assistance in this realm. Later, as the students learn to construct their own two- and three-dimensional figures, the activities Cardboard Strip Geometry, Aluminum Foil Geometry, and String Geometry will be both interesting and challenging. Three additional activities—Classroom Geometry Search, That's Mine, and Geo-Search—will allow students to experience both artistic and functional geometry that has been utilized in their surroundings. Finally, the students may make use of geometric and measurement concepts when Constructing and Using a Hypsometer.

Certain activities from other chapters of this book may also be adapted for use with geometry. Some of these are Primary Dominoes and Box Puzzles from Chapter I, Bean Toss Subtraction in Chapter IV, Multiplication Grid Diagrams in Chapter V, Math File Folders and Checkerboard Math in Chapter VIII, as well as Measure My House, Measurement Madness, Go Fly a Paper Airplane, and Take Me to Your Litre from Chapter XI.

◎◉◎◉◎◉◎◉◎◉◎◉◎◉◎◉◎◉◎◉◎◉◎◉◎

SORT THE SHAPES

(grades k–3)

purposes

To help children to learn the characteristics of basic geometric shapes

To assist students in sorting geometric shapes according to their attributes

preparation

Obtain four empty cans and felt material of four different colors. Cover each can with a different colored felt. Also cut triangle, square, circle, and rectangle-shaped pieces, of all four colors, from the remaining felt. For beginners, these shapes should all be approximately the same size. For more advanced students, another attribute may be added by cutting figures of two or three sizes.

directions

Ask the students to sort the shapes into their appropriate can according to color; thus, the red shapes should go into the red can, blue shapes in the blue can, etc. Then ask them what geometric-shaped pieces there are in each can. As they are emptied it can be confirmed that there are circles, squares, triangles, and rectangles.

Now designate a can for each shape by placing a figure on the outside of each can (felt will adhere to felt). Instruct the children to sort the pieces according to shape only; that is, the triangles will all go into the red can that has a triangle adhered to the outside of it, etc.

Next, the students can sort the pieces according to shape and color. For example, only red squares can be put into the red can, etc. Furthermore, if the figures are of different sizes—as small, medium, and large—they might be sorted according to three attributes; as such, for example, only the large blue circles could be put into the blue can, etc.

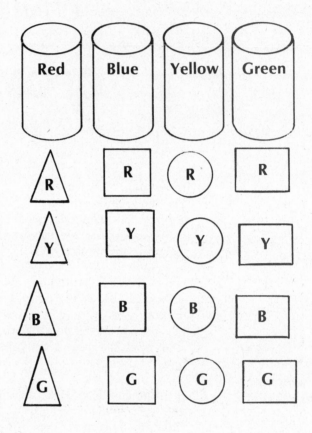

While participating in such activities the teacher also has an opportunity to assess an individual student's understanding of the characteristics of a particular geometric shape. For example, the student might be asked what a particular figure is. If she says it is a triangle, she might be asked to tell why she thinks it is a triangle. If she answers it has three sides or three angles, without prompting, she likely has an understanding of the features of a triangle. However, if the student cannot give a complete explanation of the figure's characteristics, then the teacher has an opportunity to teach or reteach as needed.

COLOR A GEOMETRIC PICTURE

(grades k-3)

purposes

To help students to identify and match congruent and similar geometric figures

To utilize color and geometry in order to complete a simple art project

Color: △ red   ▭ blue   ○ yellow

*An enlarged version of this Geometric Picture worksheet for classroom reproduction is found in Appendix B, Item 29.

preparation

You will need to prepare sufficient duplicated copies of a geometric picture (such as the illustration above) for each participating student. More pictures of this type can be readily devised by the teacher. However, if the teacher

desires assistance, many children's coloring books provide pictures that can easily be modified for classroom use. In addition to the pictures, the students will need either color crayons or paints to work with.

directions

Begin with a discussion of geometric figures that your students need to work with. Use appropriate models and ask them pertinent questions such as:

1. What figure has three edges?
2. How are a square and a rectangle different?
3. In what ways are they the same?

4. What do we mean when we say figures are similar?

Distribute the geometric pictures and instruct the students to paint or color the pictures according to the instructions listed. If they have difficulty reading the instructions, you may read them aloud. Then circulate among them and be of assistance wherever nec-

201

essary, and continue to ask questions of individual students such as, "How did you decide that the boat sail was a triangle?" When they have finished, hang their pictures for display purposes.

variations

If the students know their geometric shapes quite well, they might be asked to devise their own geometric pictures. The results will likely be very interesting; anything from race cars to animals to Indian blanket designs could happen. The geometric picture procedure can also be used in this manner with upper-grade students.

GEOMETRY bEAN bAG TOSS

(grades k–4)

purposes

To practice identifying geometric shapes

To identify plane geometry shapes as they are utilized in geometric solids

To improve the accuracy of the students' throwing skills

preparation

Obtain the top of a large cardboard box and use a sharp knife to make the desired geometric cutouts. Then bean bags of the same shape, but slightly smaller in size, will need to be sewn. Finally, if the bean bag toss is to be correlated with solid geometry, a set of related solid geometric figures (or boxes and containers that incorporate the shapes to be used) will need to be on hand.

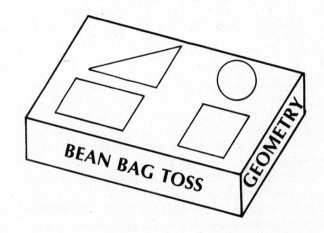

directions

Set the Geometry Bean Bag Toss box an appropriate distance from a throwing line. Then tell the students that they may score points for throwing the bean bags into the box openings. As they get ready to throw, they must tell the geometric shape of that bean bag and some attribute of it. For example, "I am going to throw a square; it has four sides of equal length." If the thrown bean bag goes into any shape cutout the student earns a point, but if it goes through the same shape (as a triangular bean bag falling through the triangle cutout), then two points are scored.

Sphere

Pyramid

Cube

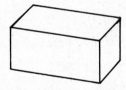

Rectangular solid

If solid geometry models (or boxes and containers that utilize the Bean Bag Toss box cutouts in their design) are available the identification process can be carried out a step further. To do so, ask the student to identify the solid model(s) that makes use of the cutout shape in its design; for example, the square is the same as one face of the cube, etc. If the identification is made correctly, the student can also score an additional point. Thus, the process now becomes one of correlating plane and solid geometry.

cardboard strip geometry

(grades k–8)

purposes

To construct the frameworks for two- and three-dimensional geometric figures

To discover applied uses in the everyday world for geometric frameworks

preparation

Use heavy-weight cardboard (not corrugated) or poster board to make fifty long and twenty-five short strips as illustrated. The longer strips should be approximately 12 inches in length, the shorter ones 6 inches, and a few of other assorted lengths. Then use a paper punch to make holes in the ends of each strip. Finally, about 200 paper fasteners will be needed.

directions

At the onset have the students experiment with the cardboard strips and paper fasteners to see how many different two-dimensional shapes they can construct and name. They will no doubt come up with several types of triangles, rectangles, pentagons, etc.

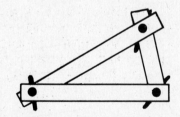

A triangular framework is "stable."

After a time the students will likely notice that the triangular frameworks are "firm" or "stable." That is, when you push on an edge or vertex a triangle retains the same shape. However, other figures do not. For example, when the edge or vertex of a rectangle is pushed the framework tends to lean or collapse.

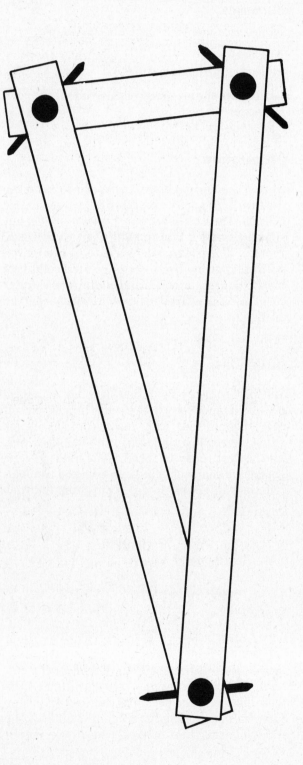

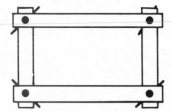
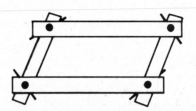

A rectangular framework is "nonstable."

At this point ask the students if they could "firm up" the rectangle (or any framework other than a triangle) so that it would become "stable." Their constructions would tend to look something like the two illustrations below.

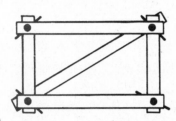

The rectangular framework is now "stable."

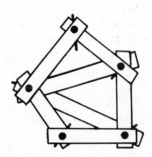

The "supports" caused the pentagon to become "stable."

The students will soon notice, or the teacher can point out, that in order to make any framework "stable" triangular braces had to be attached to each. Thus, any larger figure actually became a series of smaller triangles insofar as "stable" support was concerned.

Once the students have grasped the concept of triangulation, as a strength factor, have them relate it to the construction of homes, bridges, etc. The roofs of many houses are supported by triangle frameworks, the walls gener-

ally utilize triangular crosspieces (look at the inside framework of an unfinished garage wall), many bridges have exposed exterior triangular frameworks, and even the gates of wood fences are stronger when constructed with a triangular brace. Thus, by using cardboard strips and paper fasteners the students can simulate the frameworks of many two-dimensional figures and, in particular, the applied use of triangle frameworks for everyday construction becomes most evident.

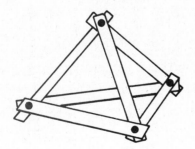

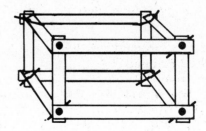

One further utilization of the cardboard strips and paper fasteners is for the construction of three-dimensional frameworks. Two such constructions are pictured in the illustration above. During this process the ends of some of the strips do get bent and a few even tear out at the punched holes, but cardboard is inexpensive so don't be too concerned.

Frameworks of the three-dimensional type also help upper-grade students to better visualize the reverse or back side of objects. This pro-cedure has proven particularly helpful in relation to three-dimensional drawings where there is no opportunity to actually manipulate or see the other side of an object.

Cardboard Strip Geometry has been found to be a versatile teaching aid. The strips and paper fasteners can be utilized in the teaching of plane and solid geometry as well as applied to everyday construction concepts. Yet, in spite of all of this, they cost very little to obtain.

CLASSROOM GEOMETRY SEARCH

(grades 3–8)

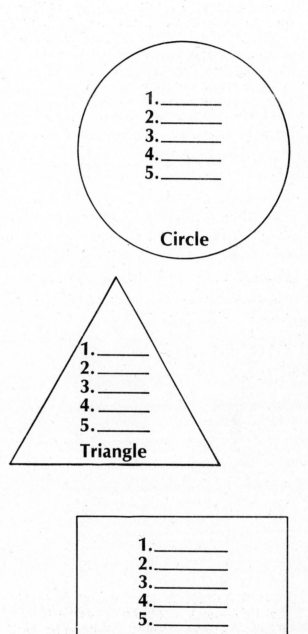

purposes

To identify plane or solid geometric forms in the classroom

To determine which of the geometric forms have functional purposes as opposed to those that are just for display or decoration

preparation

Cut enough circles (6" diameter), triangles (6" base), and rectangles (4" X 6") so that every student can have one of each.

directions

Distribute the circles, rectangles, and triangles to the students and instruct them to label each figure (see illustration). Tell the students that they are going to search the classroom (perhaps for a specified time) for geometric figures. As they locate any figure within the room that is a triangle, circle, or a rectangle they should write its name on their paper form of the same type. Ask them also to put a + next to each item that has a functional use, whereas no mark will be needed by an item that is simply for display or decoration.

If competition is desired, a point system might be ascribed to the Classroom Geometry Search. One point might be allowed for each plane figure, two points for a solid geometry form, and three points for each functional shape located. However, each geometric figure should only be counted in one category.

When the search is completed, take time for a classroom discussion relating to the shapes located. Be certain the students note that triangles sometimes appear quite different even though they all have three sides, the dimensions of rectangles can be quite varied, and circles always have the same appearance regardless of their size, etc. Finally, when the functional aspects of certain geometric forms are discussed, the teacher may have to moderate in the event of any dispute. For example, a sphere-shaped pencil holder may appear largely decorative, but it does serve the function of holding pencils so that they may be located easily.

variation

After completing a Classroom Geometry Search, the student might complete a similar search in other locations. For example, after shapes have been designated, the students could find their uses at home, at a construction site, in the grocery store, etc. You might further consider such things as why most products are packaged for shipping in rectangular containers or why most internal parts of a gasoline engine are circular.

aluminum foil GEOMETRY

(grades 3–8)

purposes

To construct patterns for three-dimensional geometric figures

To discover likenesses and differences as well as relationships between length and width and between the numbers of faces, edges, and vertices of solid geometry models

To utilize some of the aluminum foil patterns for purposes of recreation and art

Triangular pyramid

Triangular pyramid pattern

preparation

One or two rolls of "kitchen type" aluminum foil, scissors, pencils and paper, plus a variety of solid three-dimensional shapes—cube, rectangular prism, triangular pyramid, other polyhedron—will be needed.

directions

Have the students cover a three-dimensional shape with aluminum foil and carefully crease the foil along each of the figure's edges. Then remove the foil and cut the pattern out with scissors; be certain to leave the adjoining pattern faces attached to the base (see triangular pyramid example illustrated above). Lay the pattern flat on a desk and examine it. Identify the shape of each of the faces, notice the size of each face in relation to the others, and discuss any likenesses or differences. Refold the aluminum foil pattern again to make the original shape and see if there is a relationship between the number of faces, edges, and vertices.

Whereas some logical thinking has been nec-

essary thus far with Aluminum Foil Geometry, the process might be extended further. For example, if we consider the foil pattern for a cube, there are a number of ways that it could be cut and folded so that it could be reassembled. Ask the students to cut their cube patterns into six separate squares (see illustration below). Then have them experiment to find all of the possible ways in which the cube pattern could have been cut out for reassembly. Notice, however, that in each case at least one edge must be touching. They should also make a sketch of each pattern tried and note each one that worked. Here are some of the solutions (marked "yes") as well as some that did not work (marked "no"):

Cube

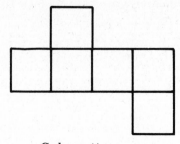

Cube pattern—yes

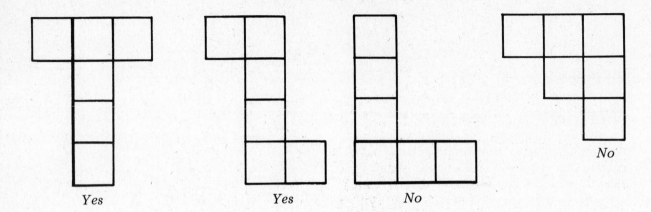

Yes   Yes   No   No

In still another situation, the students might be asked to match drawings of three-dimensional objects with both the solid geometry model and the aluminum foil pattern for it. This process, if repeated periodically, will help to develop students' perception skills.

Finally, the foil patterns may be trimmed to make mobiles or attractive Christmas decorations. To construct art projects of this type, simply cut out the center of each of the pattern faces and leave some extra tabs that can be folded over. Examples of this type are illustrated below:

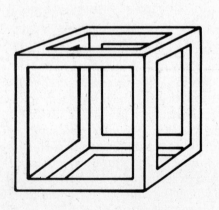

THAT'S MINE

(grades 3–8)

purpose

To match plane or solid geometric forms with their respective definitions

preparation

Secure two decks of blank playing cards (or cut 3" × 5" index cards in half). Use a permanent marking pen to write definitions on one deck of cards and illustrate the other with matching plane or solid geometric forms.

directions

That's Mine is a card game for two to six players. The dealer shuffles the two decks separately and passes out the geometric form cards to the players. The definition card deck is placed face down in the center of the table. Starting with the dealer, the players take turns reading each definition card aloud.

If the player reading the definition card has a matching geometric card, he states "That's Mine" and lays the two cards in front of him. However, if he has no matching card he says "No Match," and the first other player with a matching card to call out "That's Mine" gets to take the two cards. The player to lay down all of his cards first is the winner.

variation

The leader could deal out the definition cards. Then, as a geometric form card is held up, it must be matched. The first player to state "That's Mine," and produce the matching definition, can lay the pair down. The first player to play all of his cards out of his hand wins.

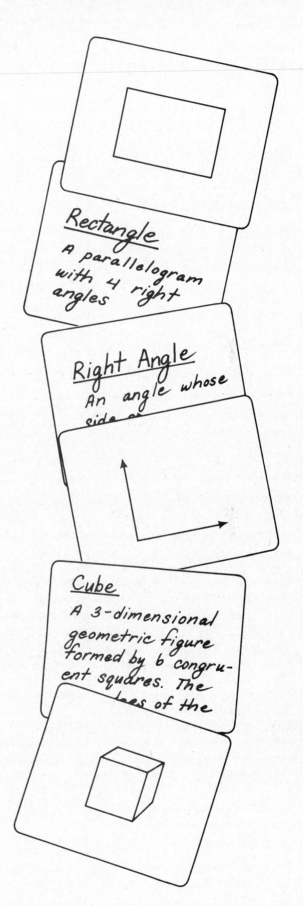

211

STRING GEOMETRY

(grades 4–8)

purposes

To construct string and tape models of similar and congruent triangles as well as other figures

To identify and label the edges, their midpoints, and the vertices of triangles

preparation

You will need a ball of string (about 3 yards for each group of students), masking tape, a pencil, and scissors.

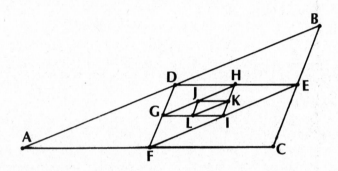

directions

Organize the class into groups of two to four students and give them a piece of string approximately 3 yards long, about 10 inches of masking tape, a pencil, and a scissors. Then instruct them to cut 1/3 to 1/2 of their string off and to tape it to some flat surface (a table top, chalkboard, the floor, etc.) in the form of any type of triangle. They should then label the vertices A, B, and C by writing in pencil on the tape at those locations (see the illustration above).

Next, have the students locate the midpoints of each edge by any means that they desire (measuring, folding string, etc.). They should then connect those points with string and label the new vertices D, E, and F. When this is completed ask, "What shapes can now be seen?"

Now find the midpoints of the new triangle DEF and use string to connect them. Label these points G, H, and I. Repeat the process one more time and label it triangle JKL. Then proceed to ask leading questions (answers are

found at the end of the section) such as:

1. How do triangles *ADF* and *DBE* compare?
2. What can be said about triangles *GHI* and *ABC*?
3. How many triangles the size of *JKL* are contained in triangle *ABC*?
4. If triangle *JKL* was subdivided one more time into triangle *MNO*, then how many triangles of that size would be included in triangle *ABC*?
5. Can you determine a rule that will tell how many of the smaller triangles will result from each successive subdivision?
6. What figures, other than triangles, are delineated by your strips?

When the students have exhausted most of the possibilities, from finding edge midpoints and connecting them to subdivide the original triangle inward, suggest that they change their focus to extending the triangle outward by multiples. To accomplish this, let us begin with triangle *PQR* (see illustration below). Then extend *PQ* to *S* so that *PQ* = *QS;* and *PR* to *T* so *PR* = *RT*.

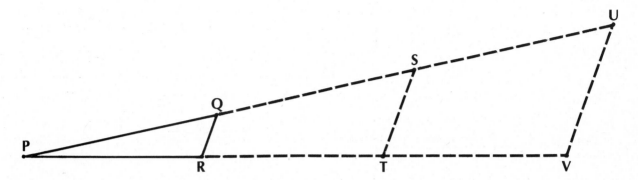

Now ask questions such as:

7. How many triangles the size of *PQR* would fit into *RQST?*
8. Triangle *PST* is how many times larger in area than triangle *PQR?*

Then extend the sides of the triangle one multiple further so that *SU* = *PQ* and *TV* = *PR*. Now proceed to ask further questions such as:

9. How many triangles the size of *PQR* would fit into triangle *PUV?*
10. Can you determine a rule that will tell us how many triangles the size of the original

one (triangle *PQR*) there will be each time you expand outward by another multiple?

Activities with string and tape have certain advantages over pencil and paper geometry constructions. For one thing they allow, in fact encourage, students to work their problems together in an everyday life type of problem-solving situation. Also, the students must handle and measure the string in a "concrete" fashion. Furthermore, the students are applying their geometric identification and labeling skills to another medium. Thus, the utilization of String Geometry for work with many geometric constructions is recommended.

GEO—SEARCH
(grades 5–8)

purposes

To locate points in coordinate planes

To reinforce the identity of geometric shapes

preparation

Duplicate enough copies of the coordinate plane grids (illustrated below are quadrant one grids) in order that each player may use two. Sets of geometric cutout shapes, of the types that the students have been studying, also need to be available for each opponent. Finally, each player will need a pencil in order that she may record her opponent's locations.

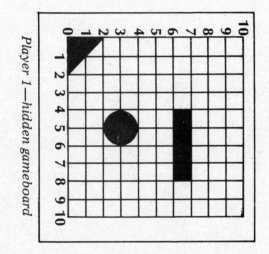

Player 1—hidden gameboard

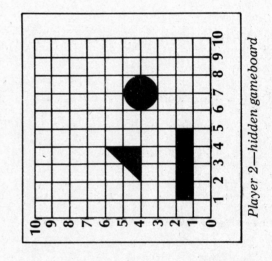

Player 2—hidden gameboard

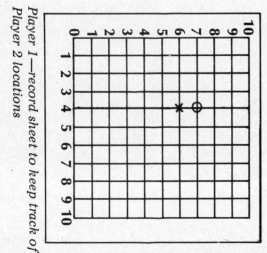

Player 1—record sheet to keep track of Player 2 locations

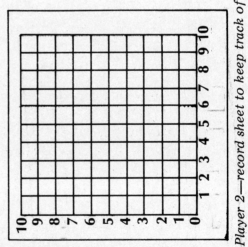

Player 2—record sheet to keep track of Player 1 locations

*See Appendix B, Item 30, for a reproducible Geo-Search grid.

214

directions

Two students, or two teams, participate in the game of Geo-Search as opponents. Each player places the geometric cutout shapes on her hidden gameboard with each shape touching at least two coordinate points.

The first player calls out a coordinate point such as (4, 6) that "hits" the upper vertex of the triangle on Player 2's hidden gameboard. Player 2 must then say "hit" and Player 1, after recording an *x* at that coordinate point on her record-keeping sheet, is then allowed another turn. On this turn Player 1 might try (4, 7) and Player 2 says "miss." Player 1 then records an *o* at that location on her record sheet, in order that she will not try that coordinate point again; and play proceeds to Player 2 who will now try to "hit" a cutout shape located on the hidden gameboard of Player 1. Geo-Search proceeds in this manner until a player thinks she can identify a shape on her opponent's hidden gameboard. If she can name the shape and all of the coordinate points that it touches, (she may refer to her record-keeping grid for this) she may claim her opponent's shape. The winner is the player who is first able to claim all of her opponent's cutout shapes.

variations

An alternate form for playing Geo-Search, which still utilizes the quadrant one grid concept, involves setting up the entire classroom as a coordinate grid plane. To do so, tape number cards to the walls (see illustration below) and set students to searching for hidden clue cards that are located according to coordinate locations. For example, tell the students that clue 1 is located at (3, 2). Searching in that locality they will find a clue card taped to the bottom of a desk that reads, "You found me—now go to (9, 0) for the next clue." At (9, 0) the second clue card is found in the chalk tray, under an eraser, and it says, "Good—now try to find the next clue at (2, 9)." Play proceeds in this manner until the last card located says something like, "Wow, your search is finished; take a short recess, but don't tell the others where I am."

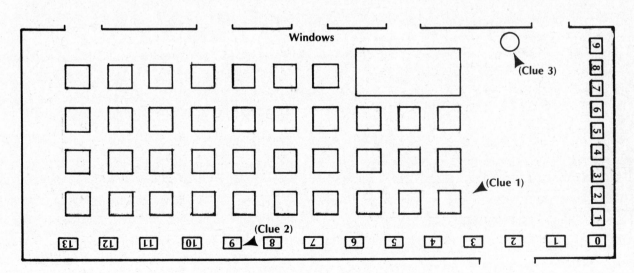

Diagram for a classroom Geo-Search

As a further alternative, keep in mind that Geo-Search might also be played, on gameboards or as a classroom search, as a four-quadrant coordinate game. To play in this manner, the coordinate playing surface would have to be extended to include negative directions (see gameboard illustrated below). In addition, the students would need to learn to plot locations as (–3, 2), (6, –4), and (–5, –2).

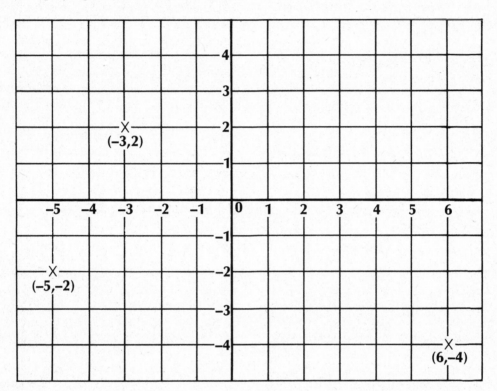

CONSTRUCTING ANd USING A hypsometer

(grades 6–8)

purposes

To apply geometry and measurement concepts to an applied height measurement process

To enforce concepts of ratio and proportion as they apply to similar right triangles

preparation

Each student will need the following materials:

1. grid or graph paper—1 sheet
2. cardboard or light plywood—approximately 10" X 12"
3. string—approximately 20"
4. weight—such as a heavy washer or nut
5. plastic straw
6. tape and glue

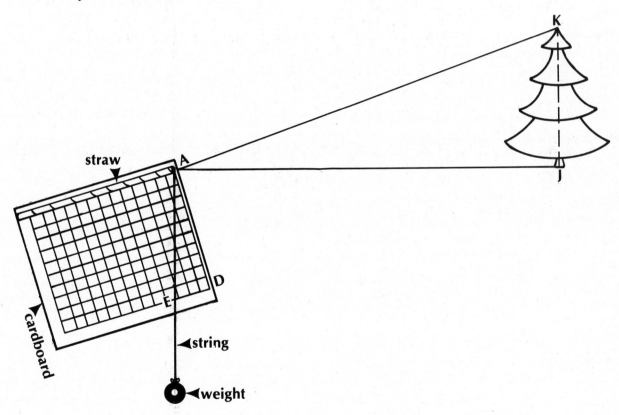

directions

Instruct the students to glue a sheet of grid paper on stiff cardboard. Next, tape a plastic straw along the upper edge of the cardboard and grid paper as shown in the illustration. Then they should also hang a weight on a piece of string from point A. They are now ready to

217

measure the height of objects by utilizing similar right triangles.

Take the completed hypsometer outdoors and use it to determine the height of a tree (or building). To do so, measure (or pace off) the distance from the tree—perhaps 10 yards. Now hold the hypsometer and sight through the straw so that the weight string hangs perpendicular to it. Then carefully tilt the device until you can site the top of the tree and clamp the string in place with your finger.

By sighting triangle *AJK,* and clamping the string in place with your finger, you automatically created a similar triangle *ADE* (as well as others) on your hypsometer grid paper. Now count off the appropriate number of grid spaces along *AD* to correlate with the measured distance from the base of the tree; in this case, 10 grid spaces to represent 10 yards. Then, count the number of spaces from point *D* to point *E* and this will represent the number of yards in height the tree is; in this case, 3 spaces to denote 3 yards. Also, be certain to add in your height, since you were likely standing and sighting from eye level when you took your hypsometer reading; thus, a person just over 2

yards (6 feet) tall would find the tree to be 3 yards + 2 yards = 5 yards tall.

The hypsometer arrangement of similar right triangles can also be indicated through ratios. Using the same illustration, we show that right triangle *ADE* is similar to right triangle *AJK* and as such:

$$\frac{AD}{DE} = \frac{AJ}{JK}$$

Then, as long as we add our sighting height to *JK*, we can be quite accurate in determining the height of the tree.

As soon as the students have grasped the concepts relating to measurement with similar right triangles, suggest that they try the procedure on objects where the heights can readily be determined. In this way they can check the accuracy of their sighting measurements. They might try the school flagpole—most can be lowered for maintenance—or a commercial building where the architect's plans can be reviewed, etc. In this manner the students will begin to understand applications for geometry in ways that surveyors, forest service personnel, and others utilize them.

SUGGESTED REFERENCES

Abruscato, Joe, and Jack Hassard. *The Whole Cosmos Catalog of Science Activities.* Santa Monica, California: Goodyear Publishing Co., 1977.

California State Board of Education. *Mathematics Framework for California Public Schools: Kindergarten through Grade Twelve.* Sacramento: California State Department of Education, 1975.

Callahan, Leroy G., and Vincent J. Glennon. *Elementary School Mathematics: A Guide to Current Research.* Washington, D.C.: Association for Supervision and Curriculum Development, 1975.

Coble, Charles R., Paul B. Hounshell, and Anne H. Adams. *Mainstreaming Science and Mathematics: Special Ideas and Activities for the Whole Class.* Santa Monica, California: Goodyear Publishing Co., 1977.

D'Augustine, Charles H. *Multiple Methods of Teaching Mathematics in the Elementary School.* New York: Harper and Row, 1973.

Davidson, Tom, and Others. *The Learning Center Book: An Integrated Approach.* Santa Monica, California: Goodyear Publishing Co., 1976.

Del Grande, John J. *Geoboards and Motion Geometry for Elementary Teachers.* Glenview, Illinois: Scott, Foresman and Co., 1972.

Dennis, J. Richard. *Fractions Are Parts of Things.* New York: Thomas Y. Crowell Co., 1971.

DeSimone, Daniel V. *Metric System: Weights and Measures* (Reprint). Chicago: World Book Encyclopedia, Field Enterprises Educational Corporation, 1976.

Dumas, Enoch. *Math Activities for Child Involvement.* Boston: Allyn and Bacon, 1971.

Earle, Richard A. *Teaching Reading and Mathematics.* Newark, Delaware: International Reading Association, 1976.

Friebel, Allen C., and Carolyn Kay Gingrich. *Math Applications Kit.* Chicago: Science Research Associates, 1971.

Gibb, Glenadine. "My Child Wants A Calculator," *NCTM Newsletter.* Reston, Virginia: National Council of Teachers of Mathematics, December 1975.

Hollister, George E., and Agnes G. Gunderson. *Teaching Arithmetic in Grades I and II.* Boston: D.C. Heath and Co., 1954.

Horne, Sylvia. *Patterns and Puzzles in Mathematics.* Sacramento: California State Department of Education, 1970.

Immerzeel, George. *Ideas and Activities for Using Calculators in the Classroom.* Dansville, New York: Instructor Publications, 1976.

Immerzeel, George. "It's 1986 and Every Student Has a Calculator." *Instructor* 85:46–51, April 1976.

Judd, Wallace. "Rx for classroom math blahs: a new case for the calculator." *Learning,* 4:41–48, March 1975.

Kaplan, Sandra N., and Others. *Change for Children: Ideas and Activities for Individualizing Learning.* Pacific Palisades, California: Goodyear Publishing Co., 1973.

Kaplan, Sandra N., Sheila K. Madsen, and Betty T. Gould. *The Big Book of Collections: Math Games and Activities.* Pacific Palisades, California: Goodyear Publishing Co., 1975.

Kennedy, Leonard M., and Ruth L. Michon. *Games for Individualizing Mathematics Learning.* Columbus, Ohio: Charles E. Merrill Publishing Co., 1973.

Knapp, Clifford E. *Outdoor Activities for Environmental Studies.* Dansville, New York: Instructor Publications, 1971.

Lawson, Ernestine M. *Introducing Children to Math.* Dansville, New York: Instructor Publications, 1970.

Linn, Charles F. *Estimation.* New York: Thomas Y. Crowell Co., 1970.

Lufkin. *The Amazing Story of Measurement.* Apex, North Carolina: Lufkin Tool Company, 1973.

suggested references

Masat, Francis E., and Charles H. Page. *Spotlight on Metric Education: A Guide to Help Educators Relate Metric Education to the Elementary (K–8) Classroom.* Glassboro, New Jersey: Curriculum Development Council for Southern New Jersey, 1975.

Mathematics Education Task Force. *In-service Guide for Teaching Measurement—Kindergarten through Grade Eight: An Introduction to the Metric System.* Sacramento: California State Department of Education, 1975.

May, Lola J. *Math With May . . . The Children's Way* (16 mm film). Ridgewood, New Jersey: Edu Kaid of Ridgewood, 1970.

NCTM Instructional Affairs Committee. "Minicalculators in Schools." *Arithmetic Teacher,* 23:72–74, January 1976.

Nuffield Mathematics Project. *Mathematics Begins.* New York: John Wiley and Sons, 1967.

Nuffield Mathematics Project. *Pictorial Representation.* New York: John Wiley and Sons, 1967.

Page, Chester H., and Paul Vigoureux, eds. *The International System of Units (SI): National Bureau of Standards Special Publication 330.* Washington, D.C.: Superintendent of Documents, U.S. Government Printing Office, 1974.

Platts, Mary E., ed. *Plus: A Handbook for Teachers of Elementary Arithmetic.* Stevensville, Michigan: Educational Service, 1964.

Riedesel, C. Alan, and Paul C. Burns. *Handbook for Exploratory and Systematic Teaching of Elementary School Mathematics.* New York: Harper and Row, 1977.

Riedesel, C. Alan. "Problem Solving: Some Suggestions from Research." *Arithmetic Teacher,* 16:54–58, January 1969.

Smith, Seaton E., and Carl A. Backman, eds. *Games and Puzzles for Elementary and Middle School Mathematics.* Reston, Virginia: National Council of Teachers of Mathematics, 1975.

Sokol, Louis F. *The Metric System* (6 filmstrips and audio cassettes). New York: Harper and Row, 1974.

Srivastava, Jane Jonas. *Weighing and Balancing.* New York: Thomas Y. Crowell Co., 1970.

Suydam, Marilyn N., and C. Alan Riedesel. *Research on Elementary Mathematics. PREP II, (ED 034 087).* Bethesda, Maryland: ERIC Document Reproduction Services, Leasco Information Products, 1970.

Suydam, Marilyn N., and J. Fred Weaver. *Addition and Subtraction with Whole Numbers, Set B, Using Research: A Key to Elementary School Mathematics, (ED 037 348).* Bethesda, Maryland: ERIC Document Reproduction Service, Leasco Information Products, 1970.

Suydam, Marilyn N., and J. Fred Weaver. *Multiplication and Division with Whole Numbers, Set B, Using Research: A Key to Elementary School Mathematics (ED 038 291).* Bethesda, Maryland: ERIC Document Reproduction Service, Leasco Information Products, 1970.

Suydam, Marilyn N., and J. Fred Weaver. *Rational Numbers: Fractions and Decimals, Set B, Using Research: A Key to Elementary School Mathematics, (ED 038 317).* Bethesda, Maryland: ERIC Document Reproduction Service, Leasco Information Products, 1970.

Taylor, Ross. "What To Do About Basic Skills in Math." *Today's Education,* 66:32–33, March–April 1977.

Trueblood, Cecil R. *Metric Measurement: Activities and Bulletin Boards.* Dansville, New York: Instructor Publications, 1973.

Wallace, Jesse D. *Going Metric—The Big Switch.* Chico, California: Jesse D. Wallace, 1078 E. 5th Avenue, 1974.

Walt Disney Products. *Donald In Mathmagicland* (16 mm film—26 minutes). Glendale, California: Walt Disney Educational Materials, 1960.

Wills III, Herbert. "Diffy," *Arithmetic Teacher,* 18:402–5, October, 1971.

Wiltsie, David H. *Skills for Everyday Living.* Bishop, California: Motivation Development, 1975.

Wisner, Robert J. *Problem Solving Strategies for Elementary Mathematics.* Glenview, Illinois: Scott, Foresman and Co.

APPENDIX A

index

title	type*				grade level									page
	G	I	S	C	K	1	2	3	4	5	6	7	8	
I. NUMBERS AND COUNTING														1
Straw Count	X	X	X	X	X	X	X	X	X					3
Primary Dominoes	X			X	X	X	X	X						4
Clothespin Cards		X	X	X	X	X	X	X						6
Noisy Boxes	X	X		X	X	X	X	X						7
Egg Carton Math		X	X	X	X	X	X	X	X	X	X	X	X	8
Math Ball	X			X	X	X	X	X	X	X	X	X	X	11
Box Puzzles	X	X	X	X	X	X	X	X	X	X	X	X	X	13
II. PLACE VALUE														15
Straw Trading	X	X		X		X	X	X	X					16
Miniplace Value Puzzles		X	X	X	X	X	X	X	X					19
Place Value War	X			X			X	X	X	X	X			21
Place Value Trip	X			X				X	X	X	X			23
Find a Million	X	X		X					X	X	X	X	X	25
Millions Race	X			X					X	X	X	X	X	27
III. ADDITION														29
Addition Bead Cards	X	X	X	X	X	X	X	X						30
Spill a Sum	X			X		X	X	X						31
Cover Up	X	X		X		X	X	X						33
Ping-Pong Throw	X	X		X		X	X	X	X					35
Penny Pitch	X	X	X	X			X	X	X	X				36
Path Boxes	X	X	X	X			X	X	X	X	X	X	X	38
Constructing 3 × 3 Magic Squares	X	X	X	X				X	X	X	X	X	X	40
Add 'Em Up	X	X	X	X					X	X	X	X	X	42
Palindromic Addition	X	X	X	X					X	X	X	X	X	43

*G—Group Tasks   I—Independent Work   S—Seatwork   C—Center Activities

*G—Group Tasks   I—Independent Work   S—Seatwork   C—Center Activities

*G—Group Tasks   I—Independent Work   S—Seatwork   C—Center Activities

APPENDIX B

worksheets, gameboards, and learning aids for reproduction

◎◎◎◎◎◎◎◎◎◎◎◎◎◎◎◎◎◎◎◎◎◎◎◎◎◎◎◎◎◎

◎◎◎◎◎◎◎◎◎◎◎◎◎◎◎◎◎◎◎◎◎◎◎◎◎◎◎◎◎◎◎◎◎◎◎◎

worksheets, gameboards, and learning aids for reproduction

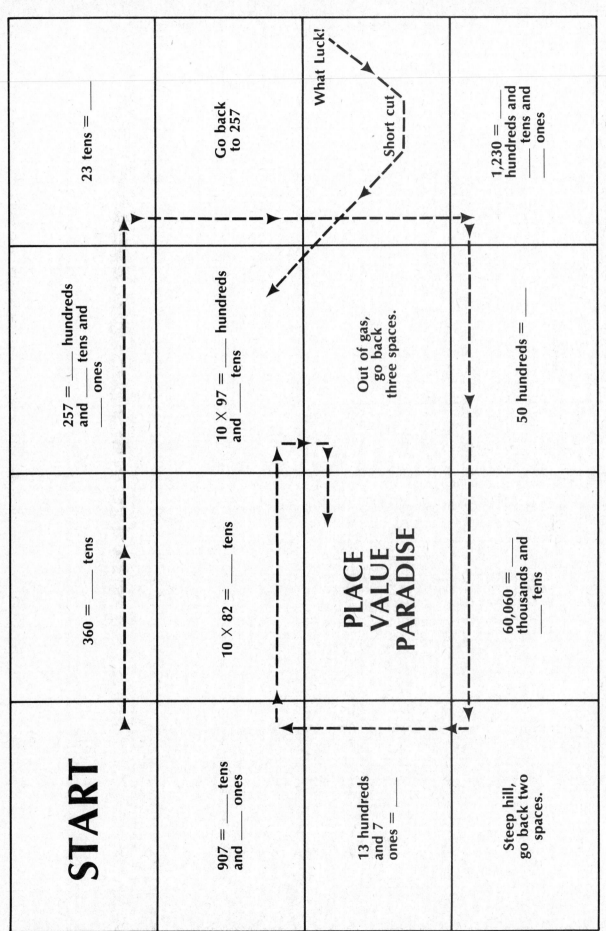

APPENDIX ITEM 1 Place Value Trip

START

360 = ____ tens

257 = ____ hundreds and ____ tens and ____ ones

23 tens = ____

907 = ____ tens and ____ ones

10 × 82 = ____ tens

10 × 97 = ____ hundreds and ____ tens

Go back to 257

What Luck!

Short cut

13 hundreds and 7 ones = ____

PLACE VALUE PARADISE

Out of gas, go back three spaces.

Steep hill, go back two spaces.

60,060 = ____ thousands and ____ tens

50 hundreds = ____

1,230 = ____ hundreds and ____ tens and ____ ones

From *Dr. Jim's Elementary Math Prescriptions*, © 1978 by Goodyear Publishing Company, Inc., Dr. James L. Overholt.

Find a Million

A. | 1 | 2 | 3 | 4 | 5 | 6 | 7 | 8 | 9 | 10 | 11 | 12 |

B. | 1 | 2 | 3 | 4 | 5 | 6 | 7 | 8 | 9 | 10 | 11 | 12 |

C. | 1 | 2 | 3 | 4 | 5 | 6 | 7 | 8 | 9 | 10 | 11 | 12 |

D. | 1 | 2 | 3 | 4 | 5 | 6 | 7 | 8 | 9 | 10 | 11 | 12 |

E. | 1 | 2 | 3 | 4 | 5 | 6 | 7 | 8 | 9 | 10 | 11 | 12 |

F. | 1 | 2 | 3 | 4 | 5 | 6 | 7 | 8 | 9 | 10 | 11 | 12 |

G. | 1 | 2 | 3 | 4 | 5 | 6 | 7 | 8 | 9 | 10 | 11 | 12 |

Game	A.	B.	C.	D.	E.	F.	G.	Grand Total
Totals								

From *Dr. Jim's Elementary Math Prescriptions*, © 1978 by Goodyear Publishing Company, Inc., Dr. James L. Overholt.

APPENDIX ITEM 4
Penny Pitch

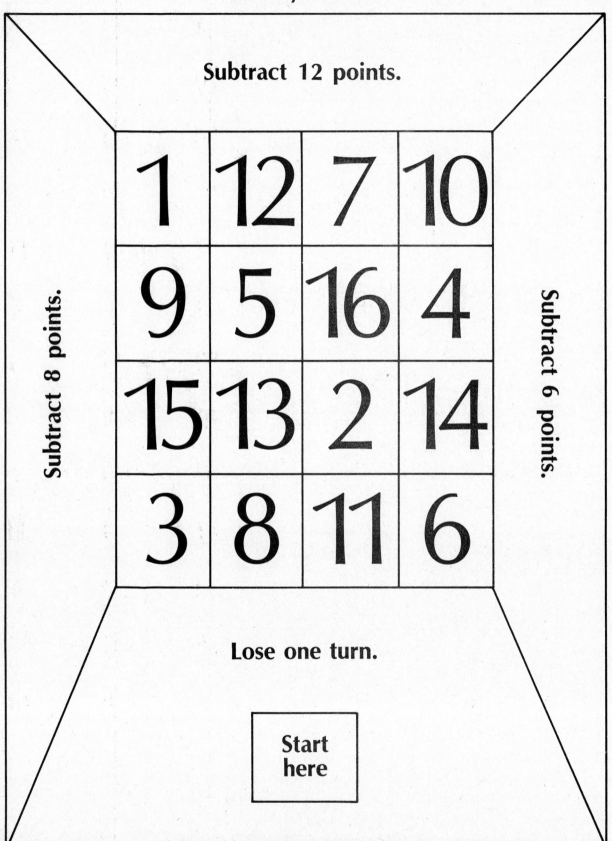

Subtract 12 points.

1	12	7	10
9	5	16	4
15	13	2	14
3	8	11	6

Subtract 8 points.

Subtract 6 points.

Lose one turn.

Start
here

From *Dr. Jim's Elementary Math Prescriptions*, © 1978 by Goodyear Publishing Company, Inc., Dr. James L. Overholt.

Punch-out Rabbit

Touch and Subtract

1	2	3	4	5	6	7	8	9	10	11	12	■
												–1
												–2
												–3
												–4
												–5
												–6
												–7
												–8
												–9
												–10
												–11
												–12

(Answer numerals – cut apart)

0

1	0

2	1	0

3	2	1	0

4	3	2	1	0

5	4	3	2	1	0

6	5	4	3	2	1	0

7	6	5	4	3	2	1	0

8	7	6	5	4	3	2	1	0

9	8	7	6	5	4	3	2	1	0

10	9	8	7	6	5	4	3	2	1	0

11	10	9	8	7	6	5	4	3	2	1	0

Subtraction or Division Squares

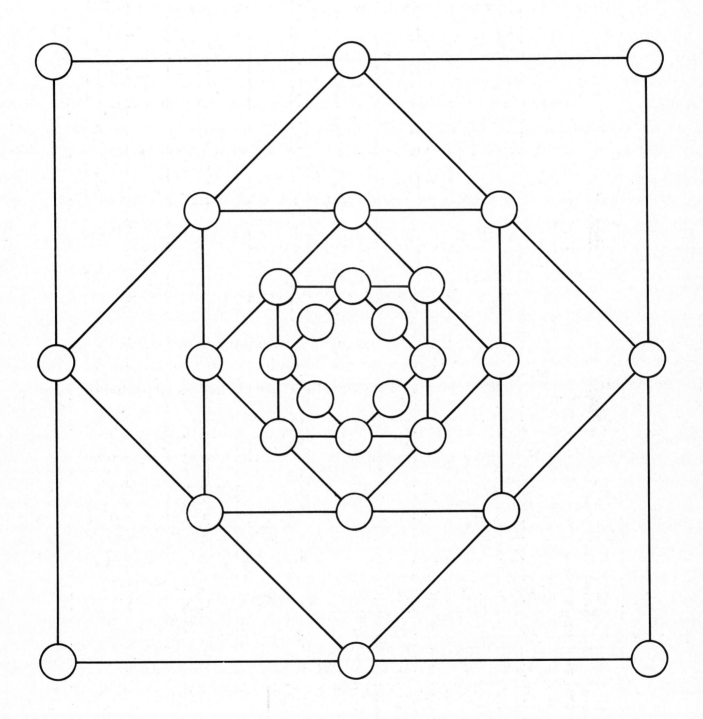

Here I Am

X	1	2	3	4	5	6	7	8	9
1									
2									
3									
4									
5									
6									
7									
8									
9									

Multo

M	U	L	T	O
		FREE		

APPENDIX ITEM 11   **Tangle Tables**

X				

X					

Divide to Get Home

112	88	9,600	382	1,001	Start
3,751	612	399	401	5,112	452
2,331	4,005	HOME	3,456	6,789	651
213	123	10,100	7,891	316	812
366	587	1,199	912	580	319
3,001	988	714	659	1,112	2,847

Number Grid

9	6	81	42	7	6	19
45	2	27	8	6	8	25
5	7	3	5	1	14	7
21	4	9	6	14	3	11
56	7	28	2	15	2	9
3	18	2	3	10	8	3
36	9	14	2	28	42	7
4	5	7	56	9	6	4
20	4	2	70	3	14	24
80	1	28	35	17	22	6
4	19	7	35	29	2	16
15	0	5	1	10	11	2
60	19	12	69	5	22	8
67	34	24	105	79	57	32

Capture a Numeral

1	11	21	31	41	51	61	71	81	91
2	12	22	32	42	52	62	72	82	92
3	13	23	33	43	53	63	73	83	93
4	14	24	34	44	54	64	74	84	94
5	15	25	35	45	55	65	75	85	95
6	16	26	36	46	56	66	76	86	96
7	17	27	37	47	57	67	77	87	97
8	18	28	38	48	58	68	78	88	98
9	19	29	39	49	59	69	79	89	99
10	20	30	40	50	60	70	80	90	100

TOTAL=

APPENDIX ITEM 15   **Operation 500**

From *Dr. Jim's Elementary Math Prescriptions.* © 1978 by Goodyear Publishing Company, Inc., Dr. James L. Overholt.

Strategy for Analyzing Word Problems

Main Idea (in your own words)

Question

Pertinent Facts

Relationship Sentence (no numbers)

Equation (number sentence)

Estimation (without computing)

Computation

Answer Sentence

Main Idea (in your own words)

Question

Pertinent Facts

Relationship Sentence (no numbers)

Equation (number sentence)

Estimation (without computing)

Computation

Answer Sentence

From *Dr. Jim's Elementary Math Prescriptions*, © 1978 by Goodyear Publishing Company, Inc., Dr. James L. Overholt.

Metre Tape and Centimetre Ruler

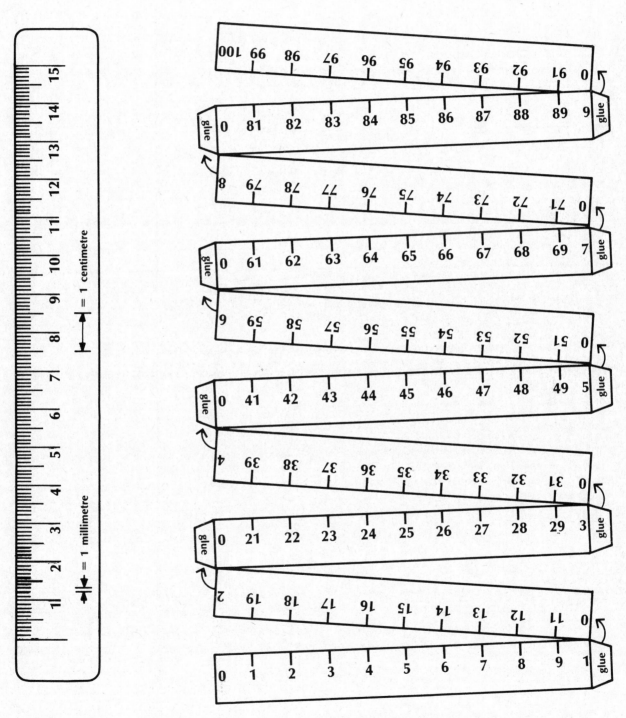

(Cut out and glue together for a metre tape.)

From *Dr. Jim's Elementary Math Prescriptions*, © 1978 by Goodyear Publishing Company, Inc., Dr. James L. Overholt.

Metric Treasure

Name _____

Look in your mother's cupboards, on grocery store shelves, or in other places to find five things that are measured metrically. Write the name of the product and its metric measurement.

product   *measurement*

_____   _____

_____   _____

_____   _____

_____   _____

_____   _____

<u>Scoring</u> (optional): The point values for different items are:

        5 points   for a cereal or food product
        4 points   for soap or cleaning products
        3 points   for medicine
        2 points   for measuring devices (diet scales, measuring cups, metre sticks, etc.)
        1 point   for any other items

<u>Rank</u>:

          25 points—very good (Superstar)
      24–15 points—good (Star)
      14–10 points—fair (Ranger)
       9–4 points—keep trying (Searcher)
       3–0 points—open your eyes (Sleeper)

Measure My House

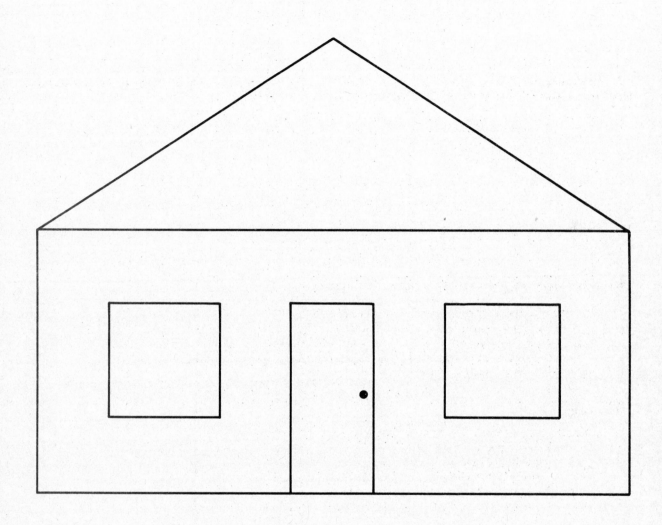

Measure the house to the nearest whole centimetre.

1. The house is _____ centimetres high.

2. The walls are _____ centimetres high.

3. The house is _____ centimetres wide.

4. The door is _____ centimetres high.

5. The windows are _____ centimetres wide.

6. Each side of the roof is _____ centimetres.

7. The doorknob is _____ centimetres from the ground.

Measure Yourself Metrically

Guess your height in centimetres. Then use your centimetre ruler or metre tape to find your true height. Find the other measurements in the same way and record them on the chart below.

	My Guess in Centimetres	The Measurement in Centimetres
waist		
neck		
height		
arm length		
foot length		
smile		

From *Dr. Jim's Elementary Math Prescriptions,* © 1978 by Goodyear Publishing Company, Inc., Dr. James L. Overholt.

Measurement Madness

Start
X

A

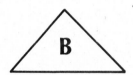

B

C

D

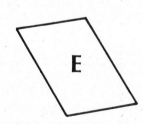

E

1	2	3	4	5	6	7	8

Go Fly a Paper Airplane

Task A—Measure the following with a metre stick:

1. Length of starting paper = _____

2. Width of starting paper = _____

Task B—Make your favorite design of paper airplane and measure:

1. Length of the plane = _____

2. Width at the tail = _____

3. Depth at the tail = _____

Bonus:

1. What is the area of the paper? _____

2. What is the perimeter? _____

3. What is the greatest distance your airplane will fly? _____

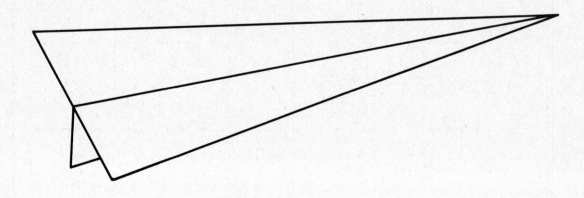

From *Dr. Jim's Elementary Math Prescriptions*, © 1978 by Goodyear Publishing Company, Inc., Dr. James L. Overholt.

Take Me to Your Litre

1/4 litre = ____ ml **Take this much**		1/2 litre = ____ ml **Take this much**	**Go down 5 spaces**		**Great . . . take 550 ml**
	Great . . . take 425 ml		**Move left 2 spaces**		**Lose 450 ml**
Sorry . . . lose 230 ml	**Move down 3 spaces**			**Wow . . . take 812 ml**	
	Sorry . . . lose 85 ml	**Go up 3 spaces**	**Take 75 ml**		**Move left 4 spaces**
	Take 300 ml	**Lose 90 ml**		**Take just 10 ml**	
Lose 50 ml	**Take 90 ml**		**Move up 4 spaces**	**Sorry . . . lose 500 ml**	
	Take 90 ml	**Move 2 spaces right**		**Wow . . . take 650 ml**	**Take 85 ml**
	Lose 200 ml		**Bad luck— lose 400 ml**		**Wow . . . take 825 ml**
START HERE		**Take 135 ml**		**Lose 125 ml**	

Blue ↑

Red →

Metric Capacity "Crossup"

ACROSS

1. 1,000 _____ = 1 litre.

4. A large pail might hold a _____.

7. $\frac{1}{10}$ of a litre = _____.

8. 1,000 litres of water would weigh a metric _____.

9. The prefix _____ means .1.

10. Sometimes you may find litre spelled as _____.

DOWN

2. 1,000 ml = 1 _____.

3. 100 litres = _____.

5. 1,000 litres = _____.

6. Litres, metres, and grams are _____ units of measure.

From *Dr. Jim's Elementary Math Prescriptions*, © 1978 by Goodyear Publishing Company, Inc., Dr. James L. Overholt.

Kilogram "Kracker"

Directions:

A. Thinking in metric terms, first estimate how much each of the following items might weigh in kilograms.

B. Then weigh each item on the metric scale to see how close you came.

C. Finally, convert each answer from kilograms to the metric weight unit noted in the last column.

1. Your pencil
2. Your ruler
3. Your eraser
4. Your crayons
5. A pair of scissors
6. A chalk eraser
7. The metre stick
8. The stapler
9. A textbook
10. Something of your choice

Estimate	Actual Weight in Kilograms	Weight in g, dag, hg, dg, cg, or mg
1. _____ kg	1. _____ kg	1. _____ g
2. _____ kg	2. _____ kg	2. _____ dag
3. _____ kg	3. _____ kg	3. _____ mg
4. _____ kg	4. _____ kg	4. _____ cg
5. _____ kg	5. _____ kg	5. _____ dg
6. _____ kg	6. _____ kg	6. _____ hg
7. _____ kg	7. _____ kg	7. _____ g
8. _____ kg	8. _____ kg	8. _____ mg
9. _____ kg	9. _____ kg	9. _____ dg
10. _____ kg	10. _____ kg	10. _____ g

Celsius Thermometers

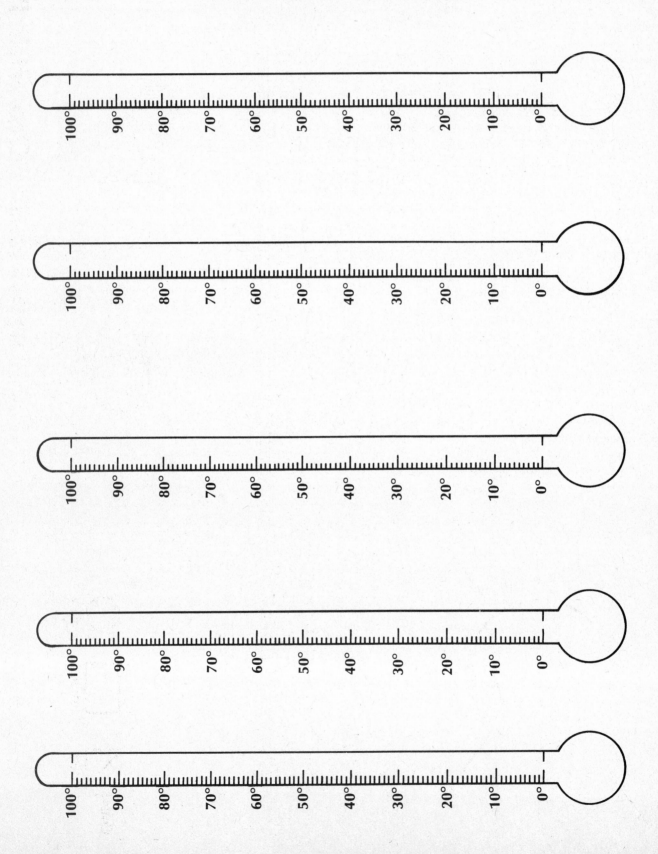

APPENDIX ITEM 29 **Geometric Picture**

Color:

red

blue

yellow

From *Dr. Jim's Elementary Math Prescriptions*, © 1978 by Goodyear Publishing Company, Inc., Dr. James L. Overholt.

APPENDIX ITEM 30
Geo-Search Grid

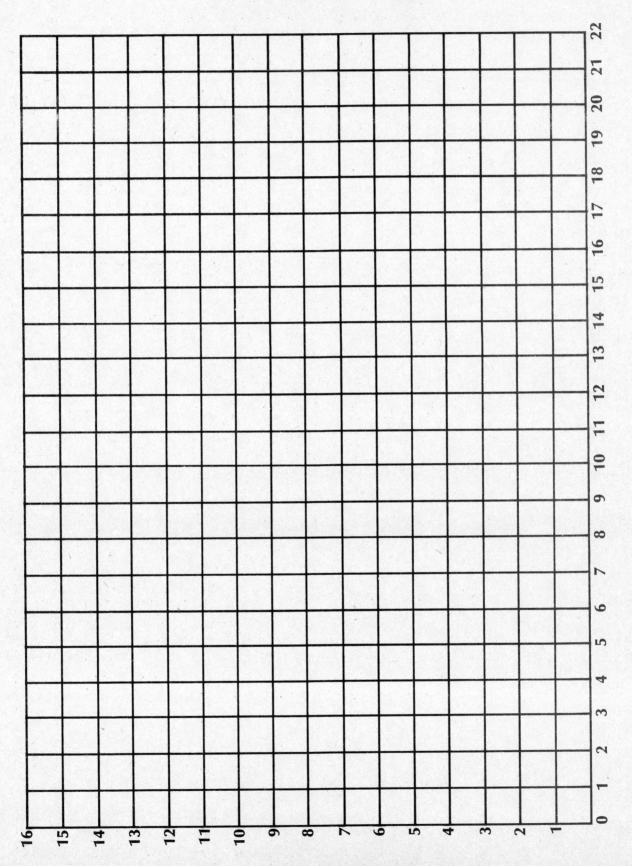

Weighing Rocks

A. Bring a rock that is about the size of a large marble into the classroom.

   1. How many grams do you think it weighs? _____ grams.

      Now weigh the rock. The weight of the rock is _____ grams.

   2. What is the rock's weight in kilograms? _____ kilograms.

      Remember: 1,000 grams = 1 kilogram
                      1 gram = .001 kilogram

B. Now bring to the classroom five different rocks that range in size from a pebble to a baseball. Can you find a rock that weighs one gram? Can you find a rock that weighs one kilogram?

   Before you weigh each rock, estimate the weight of each rock. Weigh each rock. Find the difference between the rock's weight and your guess. Record on chart below.

Rock	1	2	3	4	5
Estimate					
Weight					
Difference					

Give a Gram, Get a Kilogram

Wow ... take 700 g	Take 333 g		Oops ... you lose 600 g	Go down 2 spaces	
Lose 112 g		Wow ... take 650 g	Great ... take 380 g		Does 315 g help
	Can you win with 800 g	Oops ... you lose 112 g		Lose 35 g	Take 15 g
Sorry ... lose 550 g		Move up 2 spaces		Lose 200 g	
	Oops ... you lose 95 g		Wow ... take 300 g		Great ... take 785 g
	Lose 65 g		Move 2 spaces left		Move up 3 spaces
Move right 3 spaces		Wow ... take 300 g	Careful, take .250 kg	Move up 3 spaces	
	You get 1 g		Move up 3 spaces		Move left 4 spaces
START HERE	Sorry ... lose 10 g	Take 150 g		Lose 125 g	

Blue ↑

Red →